Stress-Free
Investing

Become a Lifetime Successful Investor while integrating Biblical Truths with the Free Market Portfolio Theory

&

Gain Financial Peace of Mind
STOP Investor Abuse

Phyllis J. Veltman Wordhouse
Maria J. Wordhouse Kuitula

WORDHOUSE PUBLICATIONS
PLYMOUTH, MICHIGAN

We dedicate this book to
our mother and grandmother

Lois Post Veltman

who taught us how to stand up
for what we believe.

Without her tenacity and role model
we would not be the
successful Christian women
we are today.

Contents

Rejoice in the LORD always.
I will say it again:
Rejoice!
Let your gentleness be evident to all.
The LORD is near.
Do not be anxious about anything,
but in everything, by prayer and petition,
with thanksgiving,
present your requests to God.
And the Peace of God,
which transcends all understanding,
will guard your hearts and your minds in
Christ Jesus.

– Philippians 4:4-7

About This Book

In 1982, God dramatically changed my (Phyllis') life and directed me to help other vulnerable women understand the *truths* about how to eliminate investing stress. However, this information isn't just for women, it is for everyone... female or male, young or old, anyone who wants to simply become a successful Investor and avoid financial abuse. We admit, our passion is to help other mature women, the most vulnerable of the vulnerable, so if it seems that this book is biased towards women, you are right, it is! Our passion is to save *all* Investors, no matter their sex, religion, marital status, size, politics, color, sexual preference, number of fingers and toes, and last but not least... baldness—one vulnerable Investor at a time. Yes, we enjoy humor... typically dry.

Nobody needs or deserves financial abuse, and you don't have to take it anymore! We hope that once you finish the book, if you want a simplified stress-free investing experience, you may never again feel the need to read financial news, magazines, investing newsletters or change your investments when the market changes. You won't even have a desire for stock tips, or to feel the need to watch the so-called investing experts on TV. You will know what you need to know and have enough information to discern investment *truths* and separate them from the myths of investing! Finally, real financial freedom!

Most people have made investment mistakes... this book reveals some of ours, some our Investors, and some others have made before turning to the Free Market Portfolio Theory. We have written this book so you will have an investment road map, therefore you don't need to experience the financial failures others have already endured. Investing mistakes can be very expensive, so save yourself lots of money and frustrations by learning from our stories. Please do not repeat them!

Today is the beginning of the rest of your life, and it's time to get a handle on what you want to accomplish. We will first look at determining your dreams and goals, avoiding investment abuse, and then do a quick overview on a key financial topic, retirement planning. Then we follow up with the one of the easiest ways for you to invest without stress, a strategy that you will possibly *never again* feel you have to change. Chapter 5 is an "big picture" overview of the Four-Step Investing Process and Chapter 6 gives you additional information for the more analytical Investor. In Chapter 7, you will be given questions to ask your current Advisor to find out if he is right for your investment philosophy, or if you need to find a Free Market Coach.

Wouldn't it be nice to be all set for life? Never again feel investment stress, the need to change investments, or feel you made a bad investment decision! This book will show you a simple way to be a successful stress-free Investor, and save money and time in the process! It's all possible and under your control, if you want it to be.

We have purposely kept the book "light", so you can read it quickly and share it with others. No matter what level of financial knowledge you possess, this book will speak to you. Especially if you have lost money, suffered through difficult markets, prefer not to look at your investment statements, or feel others are financially smarter than you. Think of us as your Coaches*, your money teachers and financial sisters. We are going to show you the way to become a lifelong successful Investor.

How would you feel if you never again felt that you were outside the information loop? Truthfully, once you read this book, you won't want to be *in* the typical financial information loop; it's full of confusing untruths, half-truths, abuse, and scam artists! Scripture warns us against using oppression and cruelty in amassing wealth (1 Timothy 6:10). Yes, your faith is very important for you to understand the *truths* of investing. Did you ever wonder why Jesus talked more about money than any other topic, including heaven, hell, and faith? Your money beliefs and behaviors tell others a lot about you.

This book is for people who know they need to invest but are confused by all the conflicting messages they hear, and they don't know how to invest or whom to trust. They don't want to read financial newspapers, don't want to watch financial TV programs, don't want to pick stocks, don't want to trade in and out of the market, and don't want to pay lots of investment costs.

This book is *not* for Investors who are closed-minded, feel they know all about investing, focus on returns and outsmarting their peers, and prefer the excitement of gambling and speculating by frequent buying and selling—called 'active trading'.

Many times, we have spoken at Christian Women's Conferences and women ask, "What about me? I don't know whom to trust. I have no idea of how investing works or what is right for me. I have no idea what an asset class is, let alone how many asset classes I'm invested in, or how much my investments are costing me. Am I too old to change? I don't have much money, but I do want to give to my favorite ministries. How can I be sure I'll have enough money to retire and also be able to give some away to the poor?"

Ladies, this book is for you and your loved ones! It's up to you... yes, you live in the USA and enjoy freedom of choice! Your country's freedoms were created and dearly paid for by your ancestors, and now it is time for you to stand up for your freedom of choice in investing, not only for yourself, but also for your future descendants.

Please share this book with your loved ones, along with all the financial information pertaining to your family. *Now!* Not next week, *today*. Next week you might be in heaven, and that isn't going to help your spouse, daughter, sister, or mother avoid scams, and invest wisely. Everyone in your household needs to know what you are learning, so please ask them to join you on this journey to financial freedom and independence. Please also include your teenagers and young adults.

Yes, it is appropriate for teenagers too, especially before they get their first job and first paycheck. Share with them now, before they get misinformed! Do them a huge life-changing favor; give them their own copy. Every high school and college senior needs this information. Future Investors need to hear about this alternative way to invest as young as possible, so they know they have a choice! We wish we had this knowledge when we were working at our first jobs!

We have a passion for Investors of all ages who are financially malnourished. They might have sufficient resources, but they don't know where to start to help themselves to obtain financial freedom. We want to teach Investors in this deep frustrating rut to climb out and get free from their obstacles.

And for you senior citizens, you are *not* too old to change. The oldest person we have helped move to this philosophy was 95 years young! Your legacy starts now, while you are alive! Help relieve investment abuse for your family and future generations, one Investor at a time...*forever*!

Your behaviors are determined by your beliefs, your faith, and are huge determinants of your life's successes. We are Christians and integrate our faith into our whole life stewardship behaviors, including investing. We encourage you to do the same. So many scripture passages apply to our topic that there isn't room for them all, therefore some places we just listed some of the verses. We apologize that we couldn't use all the appropriate passages, so feel free to add your own to each section. Moreover, we periodically felt the need to repeat information; as educators, we realize that even the smartest of minds need repetition.

If you want to be a good steward, a manager, or trustee of all the assets God has blessed you with, read on. If not, we wish you a good life, and ask that you pass this book on to someone who wants to fulfill the Parable of the Talents' mandate to use and grow your God-given talents.

Of course, you do not need to be a follower of Christ to believe in the Free Market Portfolio Theory, however we feel integrating scripture and investment beliefs makes one's faith and behaviors even stronger. We have non-Christian Investors, and they prefer this efficient philosophy due to its integrity and practicality. If you are willing to learn a new way to invest, you will see a lot of common sense in the Free Markets philosophy.

Are you ready to let go of your old money stresses? It takes courage to make changes. Courage is not the absence of fear; it is being scared but still taking the next step. We will help you find courage and enjoyment while changing your life and securing your own peace of mind and financial freedom.

Welcome to the *Stress-Free Investing* journey! We pray it will be an awakening!

Notes*

1. We use the term 'Advisor' to mean all commission based sales persons, such as, but not limited to: Stockbrokers, Financial Planners, Registered Representatives, and Insurance Agents.

2. We use the term 'Coach' to mean fee-only or fee-based Free Market Coaches, such as, but not limited to: Investment Advisory Representatives of Registered Investment Advisors, Wealth Coaches, Investment Coaches, Investment Advisors, and Financial Coaches.

3. We use the term 'Investor' to mean all Clients, who pay fees and/or commissions.

4. All stories are true; however, Investor names have been changed except for Maria, Phyllis and Jerry! We have made the mistakes, so you don't have to!

5. Most Advisors are male; therefore, we will represent all Advisors with male references rather than s/he.

6. Stop worrying! Start enjoying your blessings.

> **Be very careful, then, how you live—not as unwise but as wise, making the most of every opportunity, because the days are evil. Therefore do not be foolish, but understand what the LORD's will is.**
>
> **– Ephesians 5:15-17 (NIV)**

1

STOP the Stress!

*Banish anxiety from your heart and cast
off the troubles of your body*

— Ecclesiastes 11:10

Feeling Out of the Information Loop?

Have you ever thought that everybody else knows something you should know, but don't? Guess what, some people do know something you don't... plus, they don't want you to know.

Have you ever felt that your Advisors are talking down to you, talking over your head, talking around you instead of talking directly to you? You are right, especially when it comes to money. In addition, their investment company's advertisements on TV claim that they are the financial experts who listen to you! Really?

Do you ever think that investing is so confusing and difficult to understand that you need someone else to do it for you? Yes, it can be confusing and complex, but it does not have to be. Successful investing can be simplified when it incorporates a lot of common sense.

Are you afraid you don't have enough money to retire, and that you might have to become a store greeter until you die, flip hamburgers, or worse, turn into a bag lady? This could happen to you if you don't take control of your Investment Philosophy (what you believe) you're your investment strategy (actions to take to fulfill your beliefs) as soon as possible, because time is your friend! If you procrastinate, time can also become your worst enemy.

Do you want to stop worrying about what you don't know and learn how to improve your quality of life? Worry is a waste of your precious time! By the time you finish Chapter 6, we feel you will have the knowledge you need in order to decide if you want to eliminate your financial worries. Especially those concerns about your feelings of being "out of the loop" or on information overload!

You already know that if you want different results, you need different beliefs, actions, and behaviors. Change is possible if you stay open to instruction. We encourage you to teach your multi-generational loved ones what you are learning. You can change their lives also!

For I have chosen him, so that he will direct his children and his household after him to keep the way of the LORD by doing what is right and just, so that the LORD will bring about for Abraham what he has promised him.

– Genesis 18:19

If you want a stress-free financial future for your family, it is up to you. There are many investment strategies you could use, however do not use techniques that do not benefit you and your family. You have the power to *stop* doing what hurts you and to prevent investment abuse right now, for your lifetime, and for the lifetimes of your future descendants. You have the right to stop the abuse and to pursue happiness. No one else can do it for you and your loved ones, so you *MUST* do it. Right now! Not next year... *now*! And we will show you how.

In addition, you will most likely never again feel you need to change your investments. If you feel that this philosophy is right for you, this could easily be the last investment philosophy and strategy you may ever need.

> *Financial education is the first step to financial freedom and independence.*

We can educate and educate and educate, but if you are looking for a resolution to your troubling investment issues, you must make a firm commitment to take action. By not making a decision and failing to take action, you will receive the same emotional and financial results you have experienced in the past. Knowing is not enough, you must apply your new knowledge. You must live it!

It really doesn't matter how much money you have. You may find this book is not about the money. It's about your behaviors. Without change, you get the same bad results. You are not hopeless or helpless! You have a choice to make for your family's future happiness and well-being.

Rich and poor have this in common:
the LORD is the Maker of them all.

– Proverbs 22:2

Your Beliefs Matter

If you read the Bible, you know everything belongs to God (I Chronicles 29:11-12, Psalm 24:1, I Corinthians 10:26), that you were created in God's image, and that God had a plan...therefore Jesus came to earth to save sinners (John 3:16). You can fulfill the role of living in His likeness by being a good steward of God's blessing, using the economic resources as He commanded. Everything you decide to do or not do makes a difference to your dignity and your relationship with God. One way to incorporate your beliefs with many of your daily financial decisions is by integrating them into the simplified stress-free investing process called the "Free Market Portfolio Theory" which we believe the Bible supports.

Remember the LORD your God, for it is he who
gives you the ability to produce wealth.

– Deuteronomy 8:18

The Free Market philosophy is a core belief that the prices of goods and services are dictated by the mutual consent of buyers and sellers. Applying this philosophy to investing is similar to applying your religious beliefs. If you have faith and believe in the *truths* in the Bible, you will act on and follow God's precepts (rules) willingly, as you know the eternal rewards and benefits are greater than we can imagine. Your faith helps change your behaviors and actions that influence your relationships and the lives of your friends and family members. Your life is the result of years of decisions, yours, your role models', and your ancestors'. You too have the power to change future generations!

The Bible is the basis for good management in many areas of your life. Money and investing are only two of those areas. Scripture contains many references regarding the use of money and attitudes towards it. Money, faith, attitudes, behaviors, and emotions are tightly integrated and entwined. You will see that when we talk about greed and investment abuse in Chapter 3.

The same is true when you follow the core beliefs of the Free Market Portfolio Theory, which we typically shorten to Free Market or Free Market philosophy. Once you see that the four rules are basically common sense, then you will understand its effectiveness on your portfolio. Your faith in the four steps will equip you to be disciplined during market changes. We hope that you apply the rules in order to receive the passive investing benefits—peace of mind, simplicity, and market results.

Many family financial decisions are made intuitively and emotionally—in other words, from the heart! Money is an emotionally packed topic, and most money decisions are made by the emotional CEO of the family, typically the female, not the bottom-line analytical number-crunching male CEO. However, emotions usually aren't a good basis for an investment decision. Therefore, women *must* know the basics of how investments work, if for no other reason than to protect themselves from making bad emotional decisions and being vulnerable to investment abuses. Keeping emotions in check is a very important factor when focusing on long-term investment goals. To avoid poor behavior, discover your investment belief and then invest accordingly to your beliefs. Your future investment decisions will be so much easier to make, as long as you know what you believe and stay disciplined.

Women need investing knowledge! Many women born before 1960 are financially "taken care of and protected" and therefore many have never felt the need or desire to become knowledgeable about investing. These are many times the "forgotten, talked down to, talked around, and ignored Investors" in the investment world, while also being a major influence on most family financial decisions.

Women, if you are not already single, plan to eventually be single. Then you will need to make your own financial decisions. So now is the time for you and your friends to learn the *truths* of investing and how critically important it is to know the Free Market investing philosophy.

Everyone has the right to know the *truth*! You have the freedom to move on from where you are currently and to improve your life. Now is the time and this is the hour. Ask God to give you the strength and courage to change your life and to help you move to another level of understanding. Reading this book is the first step towards that goal. This efficient Free Market investing philosophy can change your life, it did ours!

I can do everything through him who gives me strength.
– Philippians 4:13

You are the Steward

Let's start with the big picture. Everything belongs to God, and you are His steward. A steward, also called a manager or trustee, has an important role to play. Even though the steward doesn't own the assets, his job is to take good care of them for the owner with utmost concern and diligence. Taking care of someone else's belongings is a huge responsibility. A successful financial steward needs to understand the various risks, costs, diversification, and duplication of investment assets. However, the steward does not need to have all the answers, but he does need to know where to go to get the answers, discern the truth, and make appropriate decisions that will affect a successful outcome for the trusted assets, for the benefit of the owner. We are all spiritual beings. We want to be successful and when we get to heaven, we want to hear God say to us:

> *"Well done, good and faithful servant. You have been faithful with a few things; I will put you in charge of many things. Come and share your master's happiness!"*
> *– Matthew 25:21*

A good steward wants to accomplish his job efficiently, with contentment and happiness; therefore seeks to expand all of his talents cheerfully and with the minimum of concern and worry. In investing terms, that means receiving market returns with minimal volatility (risk) and expense. Investing does not have to be difficult, confusing or time consuming. When your actions and decisions are efficient and effortless, your quality of life also improves as stress and complexity are eliminated. If the investing steps in Chapters 5 and 6 speak to you, we believe your financial life will be transformed! You may never again be the same, because applying new knowledge can change your beliefs, your faith, which is all about following your heart and acting on your beliefs.

Eliminate Your Fears

Applied knowledge is your friend, and fear is your enemy. Many financial decisions are made out of ignorance and fear. Many fears are embedded deep in our subconscious due to previous experiences, emotions, perceptions, misinformation, and lack of knowledge. Fear can stop you in your tracks and cause you to "freeze up" and do absolutely nothing! It can even cause you to deny reality. Here are some of the emotional problems Investors have come to us with:

- Not smart enough to understand finances
- Investing is too complicated
- Wants to be taken care of by others
- Doesn't have enough money to bother with
- Indecisive... deciding not to decide
- Invests too safely
- Fears repeating previous negative experiences
- Having all my eggs in one basket
- Fears the unknown
- Thinks God prefers poverty, confusing humility over wealth

So why are they not following their dreams by walking their talk? Some women willingly give up their control by abdicating finances to someone else, including their spouse. The easiest way to avoid investment fear is to let someone else make your investment decisions for you. Having someone else do your investing creates an illusion of security, but it also leads to a loss of independence, loss of control, and a loss of freedom. Most of our female Investors want freedom and security, but fear can paralyze them and keep them from taking action.

This book helps you understand that you can have control when you have the right information. You will not suffer from information overload, we promise!

We desire that the women of today be as strong and committed to the scriptural teachings as the women of the Bible. All you have to do is ask for what you need (James 4:2) and God will provide. If you would like to read more about faithful able women of Biblical times, such as Eve Rebekah, Sarah, Miriam, Deborah, Esther, Mary, and others, we suggest you read *The Remarkable Women of the Bible*, by Elizabeth George, listed in the back on our Book & DVD List.

Moreover, you cannot afford ignorance. What is more expensive, knowledge or ignorance? The answer is ignorance! Application of knowledge helps you avoid many common mistakes and abuses. From today forward, you can save money by accepting the Free Market philosophy and applying its steps. However, before you can implement this, you need to learn the basics.

> *The bottom line is that it doesn't matter if a woman works in the home or outside the home; whatever her unique situation, she must be involved in all the family's financial matters and decisions.*

You can save a lot of expenses (money) and gain a lot of peace of mind (avoid a lot of worry) if you decide to believe. You don't need to know all the details, just the concept, and understand the "Four-Step Investing Process."

Women, please don't abdicate your responsibilities and your position of importance, especially in the realm of finances and investing. Investing does not need to be complicated. Investing has been made complicated by those who have the most to gain from complexity, and these are the people you must avoid! We'll teach you how to avoid complexity and keep it simple.

Stop worrying, you can learn this. You know that change is necessary to get different results... now we'll show you how!

> *But seek first his kingdom and his righteousness, and all these things will be given to you as well. Therefore do not worry about tomorrow, for tomorrow will worry about itself. Each day has enough trouble of its own.*
>
> *— Matthew 6:33-34*

2

No Regrets!

...with God all things are possible.
— Matthew 19:26

What's Right for You?

Carla was a young widow. She and her husband Tom, age 43, had three children under the age of ten when Tom unexpectedly died from a heart attack while jogging. Tom had been the financial provider and decision maker of the family, so now that Tom was gone, Carla looked to her brother to help her make her investment decisions. Within six months of Tom's death, Carla had moved 100% of her long-term growth investments to government bonds. Her family's goals hadn't changed. She still wanted to provide for her children's college and eventually retire. The problem was that she was no longer investing appropriately in order to accomplish her and Tom's previously established family goals. Carla was now listening to someone who didn't understand her goals and how investing for growth with broad global diversification actually reduces risk and attains market returns. Her brother's philosophy of investing in "safer" government bonds could not possibly fulfill Carla's goals and passions within her lifetime. Also, her change of investments did not correlate with her inner values of wanting to eventually give to her favorite ministries. Stress-free investing doesn't mean investing in bonds or getting out of the market!

Are you loyal to someone who is hurting you? Who are you listening to: financial gurus, talking heads on TV, commission Advisors, relatives, friends, or neighbors? It is possible they are talking nonsense at a maximum and don't understand the markets at a minimum. Typically they brag about the returns of a few investments, but the rest of their portfolios may be under water.

Problem is that all this "noise" is hurting you. Do you know what you want to achieve during your lifetime? Do you realize what amount of risk is required to fulfill your dreams? If not, you cannot have peace of mind and contentment that you are on the right path to success. Are your behaviors and decisions supporting your dreams, wishes, and virtues? To obtain financial peace, your actions must be positive and at the appropriate risk level to achieve your dreams and goals. There is absolutely no room for negative thinking along the path because mind games deflate your desires and take away your energy and motivation. You heard us... there is *no room* for excuses or complaints, or the phrase, "I can't!"

Who are you and what is right for you? This chapter is all about looking within yourself and discovering what you need, want, and desire. What are your beliefs, dreams, and goals? Not your spouse's goals, not your children's goals, not your parents' goals... YOUR goals. God had a plan, and worked His plan, what is your plan? If you want to be like God, listen and obey His Word. Your obedience will be rewarded. Begin your journey to stress-free investing and true happiness by answering these five questions:

1. What needs to be accomplished before the end of your lifetime, so you will have no regrets?
2. Everyone has passions, something they would like to do if they had no money concerns. What are your passions?
3. What would you do if you knew you couldn't fail? Think BIG!
4. What is God's purpose for your life? Why are you living here and now?
5. Are your current actions and decisions true to your virtues?

Here is God's plan...He also has a plan for you!

For God so loved the world that he gave his one and only Son, that whoever believes in him shall not perish but have eternal life.

– John 3:16

Integrate Your Virtues into Your Goals

In the mid-1950s, our family (Phyllis') lived in the Midwest in the church parsonage where our father was serving as the pastor. Our cultural values didn't allow us to partake in certain activities on Sundays, such as riding our bikes or swimming. What would the church members think if the we were seen sunning out on the beach or at a pool on the Lord's Day? That was just not allowed, especially for the preacher's kids! It felt like we were living in a fish bowl, and everyone was watching us to see if we made a mistake.

Many years later, my father became the pastor of a West Coast church, with a completely different church environment. When we visited my folks at their new church, the church members invited us to go swimming on Sunday. We were shocked! Now, in the 21st century when we visit our Midwest family and friends, the cultural attitudes and values have dramatically changed. Most activities are now allowed on Sunday there as well! These were values, not virtues.

Many Advisors talk about goals and values, but do not mention virtues. Do you know the difference?

Values are important; however, they change according to the culture and environment. They are subjective. We humans create them from our own opinions. On their own, values have no perception of right or wrong and are constantly evolving.

Virtues however are constant. God, not man, created them. They are objective and therefore not affected by the local environment. Virtues are commonly accepted throughout the universe and differentiate right from wrong. Virtues are what you know and believe to be right...they are always the same, never changing, no matter where you live. Examples of virtues are:

- Honesty
- Humility
- Sacrificial giving
- Working smart
- Accountability and responsibility
- Self-Control

The opposite of virtues are vices! No explanation needed.

What are your goals and virtues? Your goals, integrated with your virtues, will explain your passions and dreams so you can understand yourself better. So you don't have any regrets at the end of your life, it is very important to have your specific goals written down, as this is a critical piece of your life's road map.

> *Your written goals will help you determine how you must change and start your journey toward becoming successful.*

Change can be very difficult, but you already know that God did not come for the perfect people; he came to help the sinners. No matter what you have done in the past, God will accept you if you just ask Him. The Bible shows us that God changed things to fit His plans! If he can change the wind, he can change you too and help you accomplish your best dreams, greater than you ever thought possible.

> *He got up, rebuked the wind and said to the waves, "Quiet! Be still!" Then the wind died down and it was completely calm*
>
> *Mark 4:39*

Dream Bigger

All successes begin with your thoughts, so start dreaming big. Remember, nothing is impossible for God, so we repeat, *think your best thoughts!*

Do this life-changing step. Take a piece of paper and write down your best possible dream and passion in each of the areas of your life that is important to you, see the list later in this section. Each statement must align with your virtues; otherwise, your subconscious will be in conflict with your inner beliefs and prevent your goals from being accomplished.

Don't think about the costs or the time required to accomplish your goals, just pretend that your money and time are unlimited. Don't look at obstacles; assume you can do anything you desire.

Ask yourself this question: To have the best life possible, what would make me fulfilled? Close your eyes and visualize an "outside the box" answer with no limits. What is your dream of what you want to accomplish in each of these areas? Do you want to leave a legacy while here on this earth? If an obstacle does pop into your mind, turn it around and make it an opportunity. Keep your thinking 100% positive.

Specific goals are needed for each significant area of your life, and you need to state exactly what and when you desire to accomplish each, while on earth. By doing this and following your heart, you can eliminate all regrets at the end of your life.

An example of a retirement goal might be: "I desire to have a retirement income of $60,000 a year at the age of 66, the year I retire." Or, a career goal might be: "I desire to reduce my work hours to 20 hours a week at the age of 66 and also volunteer for Habitat for Humanity."

Step out of your comfort zone and take a step of faith. Don't get stuck in being happy with the status quo. Pick which areas of your life are important to you and write down a short but specific goal statement—which we like to call dreams—with an ending date for each area you have picked. Write down your dreams and your passions will become self-evident. You want to write these items down so you will have no regrets, as you don't want to die with your "song still in you." We suggest you pick at least four areas to write about:

1. Health
2. Family
3. Finances
4. Faith
5. Retirement
6. Career
7. Stewardship/Giving
8. Feelings: Happiness & Peace

Once all your goals are written down, you need to go beyond just thinking about each statement. Read your goal statements aloud to yourself with a positive attitude, cementing them into your subconscious. Your subconscious needs to hear you say your goals aloud, so say them like you believe you will accomplish them. You might want say your goals in front of your mirror and add passion to your voice. Your subconscious reacts to your emotions. Be careful what you ask for. It is amazing what doors your subconscious can open for you.

Once your specific goals are written down, you'll have greatly simplified your life! All future decisions will be easier to make—family, career, spiritual, social, financial, health, stewardship, relationship—as every decision will be based on your virtue statements. Every decision, at its foundation, is a spiritual decision, all relating back to your core beliefs. Your goals along with your Investment Philosophy (IP), your investment beliefs and strategy that we'll explain later, make up your road map to lifetime success! Without a personal road map, you'll wander aimlessly through life, so get this completed *now*.

The next step is to put your goals into your "Dream Book;" any notebook will do, adding pictures depicting each of your desired accomplishments.

Example: If you want a new home in the country in five years, write that goal in your Dream Book. Add a picture of a new home and write out the exact steps you'll take to obtain it. We also encourage you to post all your goal statements in your home and read them aloud daily to your subconscious. You might even want to put your goal statements next to your credit cards in your wallet so each time you take out your credit card to make a purchase, you see your goals... and hopefully think twice about whether that purchase is helping you achieve your written goals!

Each teenager and adult in your home also needs to develop their own unique goals and Dream Book, separate from all the other members of the family. No one can do it for you, and you cannot do it for anyone else. Make it an annual family affair: updating goals, updating Dream Books, and sharing them with loved ones. The more you share and brainstorm, the more your subconscious and others will support you in accomplishing your passions.

You may change your goals at any time, and we encourage you to do so. Once you start this process, you'll find that as you reach some of your goals—and you will—your world will open up new opportunities to achieve additional goals you never dreamed possible. Remember to vocalize them daily, especially each time you update your desires and dreams and as you progress toward new and revamped goals. In addition, celebrate whenever a goal is achieved! Everyone needs a cheering support system.

Now to him who is able to do immeasurably more than all we ask or imagine, according to his power that is at work within us, to him be glory in the church and in Christ Jesus throughout all generations, forever and ever! Amen.

– Ephesians 3: 20-21

Walk Your Talk

Arnold and Kate came to all our investing classes and said the "right things" about believing in the random Free Market, but their behavior didn't match their talk. In the middle of a soft market they decided to talk to a gold sales representative instead of us, their Coaches. They were told they could make much more money in gold than in their liquid globally diversified investing philosophy. Greed set in, and they decided to move a portion of their money to purchase illiquid gold bars.

When we received their call, we told them that if they were going to go ahead with this gold investment, we could no longer be their Coaches. The asset class that included gold was already covered within their multiple asset class risk levels, and by taking this action, they would be duplicating that level of risk and diminishing their prudent diversified portfolio. They had signed the Investing Covenant that they would not do active money management, plus they had completed their Investment Philosophy (IP), committing to the efficient passive investing philosophy. Now, under the heat and stress of the market being down, they were no longer acting rationally and succumbed to greed by gambling and speculating with their money. We were no longer right for them. We required them to remove all their funds from the Free Market strategy, as we only work with people who walk their talk. They needed to move their whole portfolio to an active money manager.

When complex financial investments are difficult to evaluate, it is easy for Investors and Advisors to rationalize unethical or imprudent behaviors. This couple failed their "financial stress test." They could not stay disciplined, so we had to fire them. Would your Advisor fire you if you strayed from your stated Investment Philosophy? We do! Investors are predictable, and so are retail Advisors. They chase hot markets, they chase hot managers, they forsake diversification, they panic when the market crashes and feel they need to "do" something, and they get greedy when the markets soar. It is easy to make a decision and think rationally when your head is "cool" and there are no pressures, but when you are in a difficult market and in the "hot seat," irrational behaviors are rampant. No one is perfect, and people make mistakes when they are upset or under pressure. We know Advisors who willingly did the wrong thing for their Investors because the Investor requested it. That is the kind of Advisor to avoid! Your Advisor needs to stand up to you and challenge you if he thinks your desires are inappropriate for your long-term goals, Investment Philosophy, and dreams. If your Advisor always agrees with you, ask the difficult questions. You might need to fire your Advisor!

Now that you have your written goals, are you walking your talk? Do your actions exemplify your goals? If not, why do you keep doing what you have always done and expect a different result? Many Investors have a financial goal of becoming financially free. However, their actions do not support their beliefs and desires. They are not saving monthly, not capping or reducing their expenses, nor are they investing appropriately.

When you do not make good decisions, you are not only hurting yourself, you are also harming future generations. Good and bad decisions have consequences beyond your lifetime. Parents, your children and grandchildren are watching you. You are their role model in many areas, especially in how to handle money. They are either going to appreciate or regret the ramifications of your behaviors. Even Matthew saw that the leaders were not walking their talk and warned against following their behaviors.

The teachers of the law and the Pharisees sit in Moses' seat.
So you must obey them and do everything they tell you.
But do not do what they do, for they do not practice what
they preach. They tie up heavy loads and put them on
men's shoulders, but they themselves are not willing to lift
a finger to move them.

— Matthew 23:2-4

Every decision has consequences, direct and indirect! The number one rule in economics is to look at the far-reaching secondary consequences of each decision before committing to any decision. Corporations, businesses, countries, and generations have all suffered due to shortsighted decisions! Economist Hazlitt wrote about some examples of this by saying:

- When a public job is created by a government project, a private job is destroyed.

- The government can give no financial help to business that it does not first or finally take from business.

- When the government makes loans or subsidies to businesses, to do so; it taxes successful private business in order to support unsuccessful private business.

- Government spending comes from taxes, and those taxes come from profits, which are the foundation of our economy, so the less profit there is to go around, the less non-government employment there will be.

- And yes, inflation is actually a tax!

If you or your loved ones would like more information on making economic decisions, we encourage you to read the book *Economics in One Lesson* by Henry Hazlitt and watch the DVD *The Call of the Entrepreneur* by Acton Media, both listed in our Book & DVD List.

> *The reason most Investors do not follow their desires is because they are not aware they have a choice... that there is a better way to accomplish their goals!*

They keep doing the same things repeatedly, continuing to make the same inappropriate decisions and actions due to ignorance!

Investors can be out of step with their lifetime desires, are you? Do you want market returns without risk? When the market is hot, do you want the best returns? When the market is soft, do you want to escape the market? Investors are predictably irrational. Dalbar, a highly credible research organization, has studied equity Investors since 1926. Their 2010 Quantitative Analysis of Investor Behavior research shows the average equity Investor's return at a paltry annualized 3.17% for the last twenty years, and that was before 2.80% inflation and taxes. The average equity Investor got worse returns than the average 3.84% return on Treasury Bills, for the same 20 years! Investors that timed the market actually lost money, however, in contrast, the buy and hold S&P investors enjoyed an 8.20% return during these same 20 years! This shows that the average equity Investor earns significantly less than the market, no matter what the economy. What are some Investors doing wrong?

Many Investors ask the wrong questions and seek the answers in the wrong places. Instead of asking what the economy is going to do, they need to ask how to develop a lifelong investment strategy that fulfills their goals and captures global market returns. They also need to ask how to properly diversify their portfolio to reduce overall volatility, and how much fixed income they should have for their portfolio's level of risk so they can stay disciplined for the rest of their lives and the lives of their heirs. But no, they ask, "What do you think the economy is going to do?"

Who takes advantage of Investors when they ask the wrong questions? Of course, the financial industry and the media! The problem is, Investors are not the only ones making mistakes. The media and Advisors are making the same mistakes. They also have bills to pay, children to educate, and payroll to cover, so they often tell the Investors what the Investors want to hear during these complex times instead of telling them the real investment *truths*!

Learn to ask the right questions, the difficult questions. Don't ask how much mortgage you qualify for, but ask instead how much you can afford, especially if you lose your job and are sick for two months. Just being able to qualify for a certain amount doesn't make it the right amount of debt for you. So, how are you doing in making decisions that affect your future and your family members' futures? Let's go through a few questions to help you give yourself a quick checkup.

Your Investment Check Up

1. Whom do you trust? Are you like Carla, in a "blind leading the blind" scenario?
2. Are you investing appropriately for your goals?
3. If you cannot accomplish your family's wishes and dreams, will you have regrets?
4. What are your investments costing you each year?
5. Do you know the inflation risks that come with investing too conservatively?
6. Do you want financial peace of mind, yet aren't sure what market risks you are taking?
7. Are you like Arnold and Kate, duplicating investments and diluting your portfolio's diversification?
8. Has someone sold you something you don't understand, therefore you have some confusion?
9. Is your money 100% liquid?

Can a blind man lead a blind man? Will they not both fall into a pit? A student is not above his teacher, but everyone who is fully trained will be like his teacher.

– Luke 6:39-40

Your Free Market Coach

Everyone prospers with good role models and coaching. There is no better place to look for guidance than to the source of all *truths*, God, and many scriptures speak about Advisors, yes, both good and bad!

Free Market Coaching, also called Wealth Coaching, Investment Coaching, or Financial Coaching, is a process of looking at your needs, helping you avoid bad advice, and showing you the appropriate direction for your unique dreams and goals. Everyone needs help. No one gets up in the morning hoping to fail that day. We are human and need a support system, a Coach. We want to make wise choices in every area of our lives, especially regarding accumulating wealth during all of our different life stages: schooling, working, retiring, and transferring wealth to others. Coaching is a lifetime relationship focusing on capturing your greatest opportunities and building your confidence in the market. Your children and future generations might look to you for guidance and the consequences of your behaviors will live in their memories and influence their futures. Some could use you as their role model and imitate you. What an awesome responsibility!

However, many Investors are making poor decisions, by being shortsighted and desiring immediate results. They want an easy quick fix. Mental paralysis creeps into their thought processes, thereby they decide to fail with their current investment strategy rather than accept new information and change to a better strategy. They suffer due to lack of patience and closed mindedness.

Why do all the top athletes have a Coach? They realize they need someone outside of themselves to look at their actions and beliefs and to challenge them, to open their minds to a different approach. They understand how important coaching is and that it takes time and effort. Coaching is about building your potential and focusing on the opportunities that provide the best long-term benefits based on your game plan. Just like an athlete, you need a Coach to protect you from improper behavior. Stop your suffering and work with a Coach.

Your Free Market Coach will continually review your goals with you, help you utilize your strengths and develop creative solutions to achieve your lifetime goals and opportunities. Life keeps evolving, and successful Investors need coaching support to help them focus on identifying and eliminating lifetime problems and dangers. Your life can be transformed in positive ways beyond what you could have expected just by being open to positive change! Be enthusiastic, be open-minded, it is contagious and a lot of fun.

No longer will you take the snapshot approach of financial planning, which focuses on selling investments, insurance product sales, and commissions. That part of your life is over. Coaching is about lifelong relationships, going through all your life stages together, continually progressing on your life's journey of achievement and peace of mind while enjoying ultimate happiness and contentment.

The speed of obtaining better investment performance and peace of mind has to do with how strongly you feel about gaining the benefits from making the improvements to your portfolio. Change must begin from the inside—your thoughts and beliefs must change before you can act on them. Who is your role model? Who do you want to imitate?

> *Be imitators of God, therefore, as dearly beloved children and live a life of love, just as Christ loved us and gave himself up for us as a fragrant offering and sacrifice to God.*
> *– Ephesians 5:1*

Once you apply your new knowledge and integrate it with your beliefs, only then can your investment results be different from before. Are you ready to learn an alternative way to invest? Let's start with the differences between Free Market Coaches and retail Advisors!

Advisors vs. Coaches

Here are some major differences between retail Advisors and Coaches. Free Market Coaches do not:

1. Charge commissions or suggest investments with limited liquidity, penalties or surrender charges.
2. Encourage Investors to frequently change investments; do stock picking, track record investing, or market timing.

3. Avoid showing you the *true* amount of turnovers and investment risks you are taking.
4. Set unrealistic goals by not integrating your virtues, into your goals and opportunities.
5. Crunch numbers in order to sell you something.
6. Duplicate assets in your portfolio, hampering prudent diversification.
7. Consider investments that don't stay *true* to your Investment Philosophy.
8. Give you a static financial plan that is not appropriate for your evolving lifestyle.
9. Ignore managing and controlling your investment risks.
10. Expect you to become an investment professional by reading financial magazines, books, newsletters, or watching TV gurus.
11. Give you stock tips, thereby promoting active trading, which causes increased non-tax-deductible hidden fees and results in your portfolio's underperformance.
12. Say their analysts' skills at predicting future market movements are exceptional, and talk over your head about alpha and betas, technical analysis, charting, and other technical investing jargon.

In the next chapter, we will make you more aware of some of the common problems in the financial industry and show you how to easily and simple it is to avoid them. Follow what David says in Psalm 16...how to be stress-free!

I will praise the LORD, who counsels me; even at night my heart instructs me. I have set the LORD always before me. Because he is at my right hand, I will not be shaken. Therefore my heart is glad and my tongue rejoices; my body also will rest secure.

— Psalm 16: 7-9

3

No One Deserves to be Deceived!

...know the truth, and the truth will set you FREE.

– John 8:32

Say "No" to Financial Abuse

Jerry and I (Phyllis) were deceived. "Seek and ye shall find," we were taught. However, no one ever told us that Advisors would lie and take advantage of us while we were seeking.

We were ignorant and vulnerable. Being nice to everyone definitely did not make people nice to us! They did not see "honesty as next to godliness." Why wouldn't they reciprocate our truthfulness and kindness? Did we have a lot to learn! What we didn't understand was that the Advisors we counseled with were all motivated primarily by their own enrichment, in spite of what they and their advertisements said. We now know that 60% to 80% of their training is in how to make the sale, and not in meeting the needs of the Investor. We know because we have lived that life.

We were born between 1938 and 1942 into wonderful Christian families. Our parents were well known in our church family and well respected. Jerry's dad, Gerard B. Wordhouse II, was a furrier, and for years was the clerk in their church. His mother, Martha Huizinga, was a full-time God-fearing mother

39

and homemaker. My father, Rev. Nelson L. Veltman, was a well-respected and popular Christian Reformed minister, who for many years was called Dominie, an old world title of great reverence. My mother, Lois Post Veltman, was a much-loved mother, homemaker, catechism teacher, Women's Bible Study leader and Christian schoolteacher.

They were all the salt of the earth, in every way God's children. They loved everyone and everyone loved them. We were all so happy... and blissfully ignorant! My family especially was an extremely "giving" Dutch family that entertained all the visitors that attended each church where my father was the pastor. They also fed the hobos—today's homeless—that came to the church and parsonage for food. We are sure our house was marked, as every hobo seemed to stop at our front door.

We were busy doing God's work, being His stewards. All five Veltman children attended Christian schools—elementary, high school and college. There was no excess money. It was understood that starting in middle school, all the children worked at after school jobs so we could help pay for our Christian school and college tuition. Some of the money I earned babysitting and doing house-cleaning jobs, starting in the seventh grade, went to my clothes. Being taller and bigger than my older sister Ruth, the hand-me-downs stopped about the third grade.

We didn't learn investing skills when growing up, except to work hard and pay our bills on time. We had no savings, and therefore no investing. Jerry's family was also of the old-world philosophy, where money wasn't a topic for discussion. It was one of those bedroom topics, even more forbidden than sex. So neither Jerry nor I had any training in money management or investing, except to work hard, tithe, stay on budget, and pay our bills on time.

Once we were married, Jerry went into construction sales and management, and I taught kindergarten. We both had full-time jobs and realized we needed to begin putting money away for our retirement. We were aware that we didn't know how to invest, so we searched out professionals to help us understand how to invest appropriately for our retirement and how to protect our incomes. Busy raising four children, we needed help understanding how to create wealth for the future. We realized that no one worked for free, and were fine with paying someone for investment advice. We were very trusting, ignorant, and very vulnerable. We believed the investment company's advertisements and assumed the Advisors had our best interests at heart. We believed them and took their advice. We were wrong, so very wrong!

Here is a quick synopsis of the Advisors we used. The insurance man, who was our church elder; the Certified Public Accountant (CPA), a large investment firm's stockbroker; and the Certified Financial Planner (CFP®) all had their own agendas and interests foremost. We lost a great deal of money, and even worse, investment opportunities passed us by. Time and compounding interest and appreciation were definitely not on our side.

Our insurance man put us into the wrong type of life insurance for our situation. The monthly whole life insurance premium didn't sound too bad until Jerry's company went into a financial crisis and reduced all the sales and managers' pay by 25%. The premiums made us insurance poor for many years, living from paycheck to paycheck while raising our four small children. Every penny was committed. We knew three months ahead where every paycheck was going to be spent. We had no flexibility for seven years! God forbid we had an emergency. Oh, and by the way, our insurance man was doing just fine living on his insurance commissions.

The large investment firm's stockbroker invested our money, and we never heard from him again, even when our money finally matured and became liquid. Our account must have been too small and fallen into a crack somewhere. I guess we just weren't important enough to him; besides, he had already gotten his commissions and moved on to bigger fish.

Therefore, we decided to go to someone with financial credentials. The CPA suggested investments, which never grew or appreciated. His investment suggestions only received small amounts of interest, not even enough to cover inflation after the taxes were paid. We would never be able to retire with his conservative investments.

I then attended some classes through our local school's Community Education Program, taught by a CFP®, who wanted us to switch all of our current investments and insurances into her favorite insurance-based commission products. She was adamant that we buy her investments, but we had already had a bad experience with a very large insurance company. So, what were we to do?

We were so confused! It was time for us to stop making any changes until we learned more about how to invest appropriately and according to our beliefs—our virtues. Somehow, we had to figure this out. It seemed like none of our Advisors had our family's well-being as their primary focus. They all were thinking about themselves and the profits they were making from our hard-earned money. We finally realized we had been taken advantage of, and needed to make some changes.

There had to be a better way to invest, so we decided to take our future into our own hands. We had to learn more about how investing integrated with the Christian virtues we were raised with, obtain peace of mind, eventually afford retirement, and obtain the lifestyle we desired. More about our journey later.

Do you feel you have been taken advantage of by your Advisor? None of us deserve to be deceived, lied to, duped, forgotten, avoided, scammed, or sold an inappropriate investment... *every person needs the truth* in order to make better decisions!

*Everyone who does evil hates the light, and will not come
into the light for fear that his deeds will be exposed.
But whoever lives by the truth comes into the light,
so that it may be seen plainly that what he has done has
been done through God.*

— John 3: 20-21

You Need the *Truth*

Jane came to our meeting with her adult son Peter, and said she had a letter stating that she had just won $10,000. We asked her about her goals and dreams and other pertinent questions and then asked her when she would receive her check. She pulled out the letter. It was a mass produced scam letter! It looked as if she was going to receive $10,000, but it was sent by bulk mail! No award letter would be mass-produced or sent through bulk mail.

So how do you find out the *truth*? It isn't easy until you have found or been shown the way. It took us 18 years to discover the simple process to become successful stress-free Investors. Change does not come easily. It takes persistence and discipline once you have the knowledge. A lot of knowledge comes from looking at behaviors and their consequences throughout history. Learning about what has happened to others in the past helps you avoid making the same mistakes. Therefore, this book has many stories.

It doesn't matter how smart you are or how many degrees you have, everyone can be scammed. In this chapter, we'll help you avoid some fraudulent behaviors, swindles, and scandals uninformed Investors are suckered into without their knowledge! No one can avoid them all, as every time a new law is created, more loopholes are also created. However, we want to help you avoid as many potential abusive investing problems as possible.

Start by being aware of what Advisors say and what they

43

don't say. Listen carefully and be known for asking good questions to uncover the whole *truth*. How would you feel once you retired and then learned that you were lied to during your investing life? How do you think those that invested with Bernie Madoff feel? How about the Investors who didn't even know their investments were with Madoff until their Advisor informed them after the scandal broke?

Many Advisors have limited knowledge about where they are telling their Investors to put their money. They have large files on the company stocks they recommend, but they rely on "expert analysts" higher up in the management of their broker dealer for guidance, even though the "expert analysts" have no relationship with the Investors. If the Advisors have problems, they can say they have a big file on the stock. The analysts' primary goal is to increase the profits of the broker dealer, whether or not the Investors are gaining or losing money. That's how they get the huge Wall Street bonuses we all hear about. Yes, they receive bonuses larger than their annual paychecks! Some of these analysts made $50 million a year while their company's Investors lost over $100 million the same year! Where is the sanity in that? Shouldn't employees be rewarded for positive results, not negative results?

New scandals are discovered daily. No matter where you live, a scandal is always close by. We just learned of another scheme within ten miles of our (Phyllis') SE Michigan home. A couple Advisors were putting their Investors into a Ponzi scheme similar to the Madoff scandal. Scams are not always in billions of dollars or in big metropolitan areas.

Some Advisors know better but don't care! Some Advisors know that they don't know, and still don't care! As you are aware, the government has departments to help protect you, but they cannot regulate and completely protect Investors from all fraud. Investors must know what to look for. This chapter will help you avoid many of the abuses, so please share this information. Don't let this happen to you or your loved ones!

Each of your pennies, nickels and dollars count and can make a difference to your future lifestyle.

> ***God made mankind upright,***
> ***but men have gone in search of many schemes.***
> *— Ecclesiastes 7:29*

Investment Scandals

Many Investors come to us with negative investing stories and woes. They are looking for someone to trust as they have experienced investment problems or scandals. Wherever you are, scams are a daily news item. The Michigan Office of Financial and Insurance Regulation (OFIR) put out a website release about the Top Ten Investor Traps in Michigan for 2009:

1. Senior Citizen Investment Fraud
2. Fraudulent Promissory Notes
3. Affinity Fraud
4. Ponzi Schemes
5. Real Estate Investment Schemes
6. Private Placement Offerings
7. Natural Resource Investments
8. Entertainment Investments
9. Gold Bullion Scams and Currency Scams
10. Speculative Inventions and New Products

Ken Ross, Michigan's OFIR Commissioner, reminds Investors on the OFIR website to take stock of their financial education and to arm themselves with the knowledge to sidestep these investment traps.

"In these tough economic times, scam artists aren't pulling any punches—they'll do whatever they can to get their sticky fingers in your wallet. An educated consumer's best defense against investment fraud is to keep up their financial guard 24/7."

Don't get suckered into any scams or scandals! Your time is too valuable. Most Investors don't have extra money to put into questionable investments. No one wants to be scammed, but the "almighty greed" feeds scam artists. Learn to *"follow the money"* to seek out scams. Those who manipulate Investors or the economy for their own sinful purposes are condemned (Proverbs 3:27-28, James 5:1-6). Be astute and stop being abused by scam artists and self-centered Advisors.

One of the easiest ways to stop investment scams and expensive investment costs in their tracks is very simple: avoid the active money management philosophy and strategies, such as: frequent trading of stocks, bonds and mutual funds; high turnovers; imprudent diversification; stock picking; market timing; and track record investing. We'll speak more about these practices later.

> *The more your money moves, buying or selling, the more costs you will be paying out of your account value.*

Dr. Charles Ellis, author of *Investment Policy, How to Win the Loser's Game,* listed on the Book & DVD List, stated, "The key question under the new rules of the game is this: how much better must an actively trading manager be to at least recover the cost of the portfolio turnover? The answer is daunting. Total transaction costs, which are commissions plus the spread between the bid and the ask side of the market of 2% to buy and 2% to sell are certainly not high estimates."

If you think you avoid investment expenses by using no-load mutual funds...wake up! They can easily cost more than other types of mutual funds. If no-load mutual funds' total expense ratio averages 1.19%, then add in trading and bid/ask costs, which could average a huge 4.17%, you'll see your costs can easily add up to 5.36% of your investment, inside of a so-called "no-load" mutual fund (mutual funds purchased typically through an 800# and without a commission). "No-load" mutual

funds are not load-free as you migh␣
load mutual funds have low expens␣

The active money management ␣
game. Yes, the financial industry w␣
Advisor and the broker dealer␣
company the Advisor works for, ␣
money moves, whether or not yo␣
you not only paid commissions␣
charges, which come out of your retail mutual fund asset
value. No matter if you make money or lose money, the "house"
always wins! Just like gambling at a casino but without all the
glitz, fun, and excitement. How do you think investment
companies can afford their vast TV and media advertising, fancy
offices, and fancy buildings? Who helps pay for that? You—the
Investor—unknowingly pay for that extravagance, plus a lot
more.

Read the prospectus that you are given when you invest.
Many investment costs are listed within the first few pages,
however the hidden costs are not to be found: buy/ask spreads,
market impact, delayed trades, missed trades, and opportunity
costs. These are all indirect costs you cannot quantify.

Most of these hidden charges occur within the financial
transaction process. Some of the buying and selling you'll never
see, as it isn't necessary to ask you if you want to trade within
your mutual funds! It is impossible for you to manage the
buying and selling within mutual funds unless you decide to
invest using a different philosophy and strategy. Plus, there is a
sister problem, along with all this trading comes more risks. To
be a successful Investor, you need to make sure your risks are
controlled and managed.

*No one can serve two masters. Either he will hate the one
and love the other, or he will be devoted to the one and
despise the other. You cannot serve both God and Money.*

– Matthew 6:24

ctive money management, and you stop many
ney moving" abuses, where the financial industry
you, the Investor, lose. A basic financial rule is, if
e wants it and is asking for it, it is typically the wrong
and the wrong thing to do! Don't be tempted to follow the
wd.

You don't want what the other people think they want or have. Once you apply the Free Market philosophy, you'll have a unique portfolio because you want global market returns with less risk and less cost. Your portfolio will not look like any of your friends' portfolios, as they want something different.

Money is just a tool, a tool to help you accomplish your goals. It is an object, not a relationship! As a tool, it is really quite boring. It has no favorites or prejudices and works for everyone, for good or for evil. It can help or hinder your family. The decision is yours. Investing is not about having lots of money. It is about using it for God's purpose, your lifestyle and your family's future. Money is neither your friend nor your enemy. It is the relationship people create with money that causes a lot of problems.

And there are lots of money problems! Money is a major problem in more than half of all divorces. Money cannot create happiness; it is what you do with it, and how you help others with it that creates the happiness. However, what we focus on here is how some Advisors obtain money through abusive tactics.

There are many more ways to cheat Investors today than 20 years ago. Because Advisors are human, they have all the same behavior problems their Investors have. Plus, commission based Advisors have a huge additional problem, conflicts of interest, demonstrated as follows: they make more money when money moves, moving Investors to cash when the market is soft, down, and then reinvesting for the Investors when markets are gaining; adding hot sectors to Investor accounts to sell returns;

taking advantage of Investors wanting to chase the market; peer pressure from other Advisors to become imprudent; playing the nice guy and being a Investor pleaser by not staying disciplined in the Investor's stated Investment Philosophy; and wanting immediate gratification so they can purchase their next house, airplane, car, or take an expensive broker dealer award trip. Greed and instant gratification can be a huge Advisor conflict of interest. The big question is, can applying the passive philosophy create wealth faster than the scandals, the government, and the scam artists destroy it? The answer is, *absolutely*!

If you are interested in learning more about financial scandals relating to money moving, we encourage you to read the book titled, *Brokerage Fraud* by Stoneman and Schulz, listed in the Book & DVD List. The authors list over 100 ways you can be taken advantage of and how scandals frequently result from moving money. *The more your money moves, the more potential there is for scandalous activities!*

Here is a list of some of the active money management problems the book explains:

Stock Picking	Business Man's Risk
Rookie Advisors	Bucket Shops
Kickbacks	Brokerage Unsuitability
Inside Trading	Discretionary Trading
Mismarked	Check Kiting
Limited Partnership Trailers	Option Trading
Negative Spread	Churning
Switching Mutual Funds	Life Insurance Sales
Over Concentration	Advisor Perks
Commodities	Online Collars
Limit Moves	1035 Annuity Transfers
Advisor Training	Commingling Money

Margins w/ High Interest

Order Failure

Mutual Fund Trails

Selling Away

Manipulation Schemes

No Duty Stance

Mutual Fund Breakpoints

Penny Stocks

Expense Annuities

Index Annuities

Day Trading

Puffery

Market Timing

Selective Disclosure

High Turnover

12b-1 Fees

Sellouts

Specialty Newsletters

Upfront Bonuses

System Failure

Tipping

Unauthorized Trading

Year End Push

Cold Calling

Hedge funds

Online Unsuitability

Incentive Production

Selling Short on Margin

Mark Downs

Market Manipulation

Mark Ups

Excess Opt Commissions

Advisor Paid Trips

Commodity Futures

Track Record Investing

Conflicts of Interest

Buying on Margin

Advisor Sales Contests

Contingency Fees

Contract of Adhesion

Forward Hedging

Derivatives

High Pressure Sales

Covered Call Options

Fraud

Unmanaged Risk

Poor Due Diligence

Naked Stock Options

Suitability Claims

Discovery Abuse

Exaggerated Statements

Unsupervised Advisors

Front Running

Proprietary Mutual Funds

Information Overload

Confusion & Intimidation

Bond Sales

Excessive Trading

Guarantees

Improper Execution

Margin Maintenance

Incentive Production

Everyone is vulnerable! No one is immune, even your nation's protectors! FBI agents are supposed to expose fraud, not be taken down in them. The Sept. 6-12, 2010 issue of the magazine Bloomberg Businessweek printed an article about a scam perpetrated on some of our nation's best and finest protectors. Hundreds of Immigration and Customs Enforcement (ICE), the Drug Enforcement Administration (DEA), and the Federal Bureau of Investigation (FBI) retirees and current agents were scammed in a Ponzi scheme created by Kenneth Wayne McLeod, a Florida Advisor with a large insurance company. Many of these agents met McLeod when he was invited to speak at retirement seminars sponsored by the Homeland Security entities. Many of the scammed investors lost their entire life's savings by thinking they were in a special select group of investors, who qualified for McLeod's special bond fund. However, no special bond fund has ever been found. McLeod's fund was non-existent. The SEC is still investigating this greed fed fraud.

If you are interested in reading more about large company white collar scandals, here are a few books you might enjoy: *The Smartest Guys in the Room*, by McLean & Elkind; *Confessions of a Wall Street Analyst*, by Reingold & Reingold; *Serpent on the Rock* by Eichenwald, and *The Informant* by Eichenwald, all listed on the Book & DVD List.

Do you want to avoid the McLeod and Madoff type of greedy schemes? Instead of working with Advisors who promise market beating returns and use active trading strategies, chose to work with a Free Market Coach instead. It is all about maintaining integrity and honesty.

For the love of money is a root of all kinds of evil. Some people, eager for money, have wandered from the faith and pierced themselves with many griefs.

– I Timothy 6:10

Rules to Avoid Scandals & Ponzi Schemes

Historically, Investors have not experienced a scandal or Ponzi scheme while invested in the Free Market Portfolio Theory as they follow these simple rules:

1. Be involved! Receive, read and understand your portfolio statement in order to monitor your account. Ask questions of your Advisor if there is any activity you do not understand. Never allow any of your portfolio statements to be sent to anyone else, especially not only to your Advisor.

2. Requested distributions from your investment accounts require your approval and are sent directly to your residence or your bank account, never to your Advisor.

3. Your custodian, who holds and trades your accounts, must be a third party independent custodian. A third party is a firm outside your financial Advisors' company, and also completely independent from your money manager and investment company. This third-party custodian has no vested interest in profiting from your account's investment decisions. If you are using a company that does not have a third party custodian, it most likely is a seamless revenue-making money machine and could have less accountability, as it has more opportunity to hide inappropriate behaviors.

4. Free Market Investors have four *independent* entities working for them, each completely separate and independent from the other and each has its own fees:

   a. **Free Market Coach:** Advises you directly on achieving your dreams, no commissions, no backdoor gifts and trips, just a flat agreed upon fee based on the amount of assets managed.

   b. **Free Market Money Manager:** Tells the custodian how to diversify your funds and correlates the institutional asset class mutual funds according to your desired risk level. The instructions to the custodian are the result of the established goals and virtues you have established with your Coach. He has no freedom to change your instructions. The money manager is paid an internal fee based on the amount of assets managed.

c. **Investment Company:** Develops and maintains the 20-plus institutional stock and bond asset class mutual funds the money manager uses to correlate your portfolio. There is no need to buy and sell within an asset class mutual fund as each owns the majority of one category of risk. Together, these various funds—called asset classes—are a representation of the global market within 40 plus free countries. The Investment Company is paid an internal fee based on the amount of assets managed.

d. **Custodian:** Holds your investment accounts, reports to you every time any money moves, and keeps the IRS happy by doing all the necessary IRS compliance and reporting. Think of your custodian as your accountant. The Custodian is paid a fee based on the amount of assets managed.

5. Receive your annual reports and updated prospectuses directly from your custodian—either hard copy through the mail or electronically by email. By having them sent to your Advisor or someone else, you might not receive them and then you would not be able to stay involved and read the details as to how your investment company is investing your money. If you receive no annual reports or updated prospectuses, call your Advisor and start asking questions.

6. Be able to access your independent custodian's website to learn about them and make sure they are legitimate.

7. Have a sense of healthy skepticism, as promised annual rates of return like a consistent 10%-12% are too good to be true given market conditions. The market is always fluctuating, your portfolio returns should also.

8. Scam artists make their money upfront, so avoid paying any

commissions or agreeing to any surrender fees or penalties. The Advisory fees your Coach charges are discussed before investing and tax deductible on your 1040, in Miscellaneous Deductions.

9. Don't follow the crowd, doing something just because someone says you "should." You can be a successful investor by keeping your life simple, avoiding complexity, and staying disciplined.

10. If you don't comprehend it, don't invest in it. Remember the "keep it simple" rule! Follow it religiously. Your Advisor must be able to simply explain your investment strategy in plain English.

How many of these items affect you? If any of these sounds familiar, you are very vulnerable to scandals. It's time for you to work with someone who has your same philosophy. What are your investment beliefs?

For this you can be sure: No immoral, impure or greedy person – such a man is an idolater – has any inheritance in the kingdom of Christ and of God.

– Ephesians 5:5

Investment Philosophy (IP)

James decided to move half of his money into Free Market, and the other half of his money he invested with an active money manager, thinking he was improving his diversification by not putting all his money in "one basket." But what he was really doing was duplicating what he already owned thereby doubling his expenses and diluting his diversification. James was gambling and speculating.

By hedging his bet and by not investing all his money in the same investment strategy, James was making his portfolio less effective and more costly than it needed to be, causing a lot of needless anxiety and frustration. He definitely wasn't experiencing peace of mind. James needed to make a decision— either invest 100% into active trading, or go 100% with the passive Free Market global philosophy. It is one or the other, not both.

Yes, you need an action plan! Just as God had a plan for salvation and sent his Son to fulfill His plan, you need a plan and a method, a strategy, to accomplish your plan. Plans and knowledge do not improve your situation until they are applied. Your actions all hinge on your beliefs and your commitment, so let's check them out.

> *Humility and the fear of the LORD bring*
> *wealth and honor and life.*
>
> *– Proverbs 22:4*

What do you believe about the financial market? Your written Investment Philosophy (IP) tells your Coach what your market beliefs are and the strategy to accomplish them. During this discovery process, you can decide if you want to either use either active money management or the efficient passive philosophy. The first believes markets fail and the second believes markets work. Once you develop your IP, it is easy to make future financial decisions, as it is a road map for accomplishing your goals and obtaining absolute happiness and fulfillment as a successful Investor.

If you believe in the active money management philosophy, which says that markets are predictable, then you would be comfortable with using the active strategies, methods of investing: stock picking, market timing, and track record investing. Along with those, you'll also read many financial newspapers, magazines, stock newsletters and listen and watch the media for all market predictions, which we call "information overload." Some Investors expect their Advisor to move their money between asset classes or sectors whenever he feels the

55

economy changing. Active money management is all about speculating and forecasting—trying to outperform other Investors. As explained earlier, it's a WIN-WIN-LOSE game. You try to get the hot stock tips early so you can get better returns than your friends and family. In addition, someone else is always trying to outperform your investment returns.

Have you ever been on a golf course and seen someone supposedly playing golf , but on his phone? He might easily be a person who believes in active money management and is talking to his Advisor about stock tips. Have you ever seen an Advisor who gets agitated over market movements and wants to move his Investors' money between sectors, such as utilities, financials, etc., or asset allocation classes? If so, he is a trader, a stockbroker, an active money manager.

However, if you decide to believe in the efficient Free Market philosophy, it's a WIN-WIN-WIN game! Sure, you'll get market returns, and there absolutely will be fluctuations in your account value, but as long as you stay disciplined over your lifetime, we can all receive similar returns together. Everyone WINS! Free Market Investors believe that markets are efficient and random, that we should be globally invested like the Nobel Prize winning Modern Portfolio Theory, and each portfolio must include the "Three Factor Model." We'll discuss these two strategies shortly.

> *Once you determine that the Free Market philosophy is right for you, and apply it to your portfolio, you can enjoy financial peace of mind.*

You'll own a broad global diversified portfolio, with multiple asset classes, representing the broad global market. Therefore, due its design, Investors obtain market returns with less risk and less cost.

Whatever belief you decide on, do it with all your money.

Never divide your long-term assets into conflicting investment philosophies. You'll only create stress, anxiety, and confusion for yourself and your loved ones, as you'll keep second-guessing yourself. If you think of investing as a "horse race", the Free Market Investors own all the horses in the race as this philosophy holds both stocks and bonds in the broad Free Market. It's a lifetime global investment philosophy, as we'll explain more completely later.

> *Follow my example, as I follow the example of Christ.*
> *– I Corinthians 11:1*

Four Simple Investment Questions:

- Are you buying the same stock in different mutual funds and annuities?

- How are you measuring and managing your portfolio's risk?

- Do you know what your "real investment costs" are?

- Are you receiving market returns with lower costs and lower risk?

If you cannot answer all four questions clearly, you are living in ignorance and are caught in the "Investors' Trap," experiencing a life of complexity and frustration instead of peace of mind. It is time for you to make some changes and consider the Free Market Portfolio Theory philosophy. It holds to the simplified *truths* of how the market works, and how to protect your wealth.

What if you don't change your investment philosophy? Doing nothing different hurts you in the long run, and hurts your family and loved ones. You will continue being frustrated, wondering if you could do better, and not sure of whom to trust. If you could reduce your financial stress, would you? If so, you need a better investment plan, one that avoids scandals and gives you real peace of mind, an investment plan that consistently integrates your virtues into your investment philosophy

Many highly educated Investors are still purchasing inappropriate investments that don't advance their lifetime goals. We encourage you to follow the virtuous path towards peace of mind. Through correct knowledge, you'll begin to see where greed and evil can easily slip into the investing process. Following the next investment story are some additional investments you should be aware of. Please don't slide into inappropriate investments and hurt yourself by being abused.

> *He who oppresses the poor to increase his wealth and he who gives gifts to the rich – both come to poverty.*
> *– Proverbs 22:16*

Abusive Annuities

"Did I do OK?" 58-year-old Millie asked as she proudly brought out her two-month-old annuity policy and showed it to me. I opened the policy and checked the back pages, locating her surrender penalties schedule. My heart immediately sank. She had purchased an annuity with 15% surrender charges for the first 15 years! To make myself clear, if she took a distribution out of her annuity during the first 15 years of owning it, she would be charged a 15% surrender fee each time. And this is legal! I couldn't believe my eyes and looked twice to make sure I was reading it correctly. She was used, abused and stuck. The best thing she could do now was to invest the rest of her money to work harder, or surrender now and pay the penalties, calling it "investment scam tuition." Along with avoiding active money management, please avoid abusive annuities.

How likely is it that Investors, not just Millie, might change their minds in the next 15 years? It is highly likely. As your life evolves and changes, your goals might change as well. Do not accept any surrender charges or penalties in your annuity products. Surrender charges or penalties are neither acceptable nor available in the Free Market strategies.

Millie is in a sad predicament. She invested $100,000, and if she closes the annuity anytime within 15 years, or before she is 73, there is a $15,000 penalty! That is Investor abuse and should be outlawed. This is another WIN-WIN-LOSE game. Who won and who lost? The insurance agent, who received a *huge* commission for tying up Millie's money won, as well as the insurance company won, as it profits while Millie lost the use of her illiquid money and potential global market growth.

It is the old story, applied knowledge is power, and to be a successful Investor, you need to know the *truth* and act on it. First, you need to unlearn bad information so your mind is open to new ideas. Then you can learn the right information, plus learn the right questions to ask.

It is time for Investors to seek reality in all areas of investing, including annuities with penalties and to see where their true rewards come from. Authentic happiness comes from helping others and sharing wisdom and knowledge. You will enjoy *true* contentment and happiness in your eternal rewards, not your temporal or earthly rewards. They are left behind when you graduate to heaven. As you learn this material, please share it with your loved ones, helping them also avoid financial abuse and gain true happiness.

> *But store up for yourselves treasures in heaven, where moth and rust do not destroy, and where thieves do not break in and steal. For where your treasure is, there your heart will be also.*
>
> *– Matthew 6:20-21*

Here is a quick "light" informational overview on annuities. An annuity is an insurance policy that gives you an income until you die. It isn't life insurance, it is just a promise—a written contract. Your money grows tax-deferred and is taxed at your income rate when you eventually take distributions, usually during retirement. There are no IRS early redemption penalties after the annuity's owner is age 59½. A retail/commercial annuity pays the agent a commission, typically upfront, and the annuity will have its own penalties that are determined by the insurance company writing the policy. The penalties start the date you purchase the annuity and can easily go beyond the age of 59½. The surrender charge penalties are sometimes as short as five years and can possibly be as long as 25 years.

If an annuity is right for you, consider a fee-only annuity that never has any insurance company surrender fees or penalties. Most annuities have a 10-20 day "free look" period at the beginning, where there are no costs for you to cancel the annuity and receive a full refund of your annuity premium. Take advantage of this free look "window" if you just purchased a retail annuity. You are allowed to return the annuity and receive all your money back during that time. Never sign away your right to the free look.

There are two basic types of annuity investment options: fixed annuity investments and variable annuity investments. A fixed annuity typically invests in bond portfolios for fixed income, therefore it seems like it is not subject to market risk. The variable annuity invests in mutual funds for growth and income, which definitely experiences market risk.

If you believe the US economy is going to go backwards for the rest of your life, then consider a fixed annuity. However, if you feel the economy is going to continue in its usual random manner of creating greater value, then consider the variable annuity. Because Free Market Investors believe in the random growth of the market, we'll only discuss the variable annuity.

Listen to advice and accept instruction, and in the end you will be wise. Many are the plans in a man's heart, but it is the LORD's purpose that prevails.
What a man desires is unfailing love, better to be poor than a liar. The fear of the LORD leads to life: Then one rests content, untouched by trouble.

— Proverbs 19:20-23

Annuity *Truths*

1. Annuity penalties are optional. There is no need to purchase an annuity with any penalties. If you no longer have a penalty and your investments are not getting market returns, you would be smart to do a 1035 tax-free transfer of your money to a fee annuity. However, the previous insurance company will not be happy, as it can no longer make money off your money. It is all about the bottom line. Again... *just follow the money,* you will read this frequently. The larger the penalties and the more years the insurance company ties up your money, the larger the commission your insurance agent or Advisor earns and the more money the insurance company keeps. This is a huge conflict of interest. For Millie, the 15 years of penalties guarantees the insurance company that they will make money off her annuity whether she keeps her policy with them or not. The Investor takes all the risks. This is an abusive annuity and comes from a very large insurance company that does many ads on TV. Remember, the more they advertise, the more discretionary money they have. Who pays for those ads? Investors!

2. There are more expenses hidden within the retail annuity product than in a retail mutual fund. One of the largest costs in an annuity is its mortality risk costs. The insurance company's mortality risk expenses, that annuities charge their investors, do not exist in mutual funds. This charge can add up to 1% to your annuity's total costs. Other large costs

61

are in the mutual fund investment options and the commissions of an annuity. The larger the expenses, the more money the insurance company makes! Another area of concern that results in redundant costs to the Investor is stock duplication within the annuity's mutual fund options. It makes no sense to have one growth mutual fund manager buying Pepsi stock while another is selling Pepsi. This occurs when an annuity holds several similar mutual funds with similar objectives—and most do it. You, the Investor, suffer. If there is excessive turnover, buys and sells, it is called churning, which costs you, the Investor, an average 2% to buy and 2% to sell. An annuity, which holds retail mutual funds, does not put the Investor, first. It is a WIN-WIN for the Advisor and the insurance company, but not the Investor. The costs have to be paid whether your Annuity gains in value or not, so you *lose*.

3. Never purchase equity-indexed annuities, they promise you stock market returns when the market goes up and protection from losses if the market goes down. This is a very complicated insurance product and has many hidden costs. We believe that there might be future litigation that will focus on these types of illiquid products. They are complex and have huge penalties if surrendered prematurely, so please stay away from them. Just *say "No."*

4. There is almost never a reason to annuitize! When you annuitize, you are telling the insurance company to activate the clause in the policy that pays out distributions under the terms of the policy. We advise Investors to always leave the annuity "open" so you can withdraw from it as you desire. Once you annuitize, or lock in your distributions, most insurance companies will pay you for a certain number of years, or for your life, or the life of the owner and the spouse. What if you, the owner, and your spouse both die in the same accident soon after annuitizing? Who wins? Usually

the insurance company, not the heirs!

5. *Never* put an annuity into your retirement plan at work, your Roth, or your IRA—more about this in the retirement chapter.

If you have an existing annuity, ask your Free Market Coach to do three analyses on your annuity: an investment analysis; the unique position analysis; and an overlap analysis. These reports will tell you how broad or narrow your annuity's diversification really is, if there are duplicate investments within the annuity, and if the risk you are taking is worth the return you are receiving as compared to the globally diversified portfolios. *Never* take more risks than necessary to achieve your lifetime goals.

> *Be careful that no one entices you by riches; do not let a large bribe turn you aside.*
>
> – *Job 36:18*

Complexity

Betty had her MBA and was in our investing class at the college, however, she had never been able to apply her extensive academic knowledge to her personal investments. Her training was all about how to help businesses, but not about personal application. It didn't matter that she had an advanced business degree; she still had to learn the basic investment *truths*, just like everyone else.

Here we are in the 21st century and smart college-degreed Investors still don't know how to obtain financial peace of mind. Some of the smartest Investors we have worked with have had the most terrible investment experiences. They are very intelligent, many with advanced degrees, especially those from the medical, law, business, and educational fields. Intelligence in their own area of expertise does not mean they are knowledgeable in investing. Many Investors have become involved with affinity groups and multiple high-risk complex schemes. By listening to their peers' persuading arguments, they joined them in making the same poor investment choices.

Don't be pressured into joining others in their mistakes! Avoid greed at all costs. Focuses not on yourself, but on what God wants for you, contentment and love, which you freely receive from Him by following His Word.

> *I urge you, brothers, to watch out for those who cause divisions and put obstacles in your way that are contrary to the teachings you have learned. Keep away from them. For such people are not serving our LORD Christ, but their own appetites. By smooth talk and flattery they deceive the minds of naive people.*
>
> *– Romans 16:17-18*

Have an open mind so you will learn the truths and not be naïve. You must protect yourself from future investment abuse. Here are some additional investments we suggest you avoid to eliminate many potential investment abuses and future complexity in your life. If you truly want simplicity, avoid these investments.

Avoid purchasing individual stocks. They are not diversified and by owning individual stocks, you are speculating and gambling. We will discuss more about stock picking in Chapters 5 and 6. You don't need this much excitement or these potential losses in your life.

Ignore hedge funds—you don't need the grief! They are somewhat illiquid and difficult to keep track of. If the fund changes its investment objective, and they can, it is hard to react quickly enough to get out. If they have problems, the hedge fund can stop you from liquidating your account. Moreover, the fees are typically very high and sometimes the fund even takes part of your profits. You just don't need this much risk or complexity in your life.

House funds shouldn't be considered as an investment option. They are mutual funds, also called proprietary funds, created by large broker dealers. These are the types of funds that my (Phyllis') Investors asked me to leave in 1983. These funds will have the name of the broker dealer within the fund name: such as, the ABC broker dealer will have an ABC Growth Mutual Fund. These proprietary funds are very profitable for the broker dealer, actively managed, and sold only by the Advisors of the broker dealer. House funds are typically less diversified, many times more expensive, many times pay the Advisor a bigger commission, and usually get poorer returns than even an average retail mutual fund. Just say "*No*"!

Do not purchase individual bonds and long-term bond mutual funds. If you feel you need bonds, only purchase short-term high-quality institutional asset class bond mutual funds and avoid the rest. Your Free Market money manager will pick out the right short-term bond funds for your portfolio's risk level.

Another investment category to refuse to consider is commodities. We enjoy jewelry, so we'll focus on precious metals (gold, platinum, and silver) and gems. Precious metals are beautiful creations of God so adorn yourself by wearing your jewels, gold, silver, platinum, etc. and enjoy them! Just don't invest in them.

Gold is not better than the dollar. If you really want to gamble, go with gold. The risk, volatility, of gold is higher than the S&P's risk and more similar to the risk level of small stocks. If you are not willing to hold that level of volatility, get out of gold, which has limited diversification, and move into broader globally diversified stocks for less risk. Globally diversified Investors already own gold! The asset class risk category that precious metals fit into is already covered in the 20-plus different asset classes. It makes no sense to duplicate the risk levels that this liquid strategy already covers.

When you hear a money manager, analyst, or Advisor saying any of these financial terms: highly liquid futures; forward contacts; swaps; derivatives; IPO's; hedge fund beta exposures; spiders; currency and commodity markets; hedged equity; index call options; put options; or alternatives for core solutions; immediately say, "No thanks, I am not right for your business," and leave. Your time is too valuable to spend discussing inappropriate investments. You also don't need the stress or the risk of the above complex investments.

Whatever you want to invest in: water, corn, wheat, salt, real estate, precious metals, etc. they are already in your broadly diversified portfolio no matter what sector you choose—it is all in there! Investing in them separately is just duplicating what you already own and costs you more money. It really is just that simple. The only way to beat inflation is to invest in broadly diversified equities and hold them for the long term.

Not everyone is ready for our message. Sometimes wealthy people have more money than common sense and feel they are "above" the investing rules. They just could not say "no" to trying to get wealthy quickly. Some of the Investors we have had to "fire" were our richest Investors with the best educations. They liked the excitement of the gambling and speculative active market. Here is a solution: if you really want to let go of your money so badly, there are many good ministries that can use your money to do good and benefit the widows, poor, and needy. Conquer your need for risk and fast spending by starting a monthly giving plan to a ministry of your choice.

***People who want to get rich fall into temptation and a trap
and into many foolish and harmful desires that plunge
men into ruin and destruction.***

– I Timothy 6:9

Illiquid Investments

George and Bernice were empty nesters, and they were elated because their expensive child-raising years were behind them! We worked out a plan for them to save more for retirement. However, they already had other plans. They chose to invest in illiquid investments rather than in the 100% liquid Free Market Portfolio Theory for retirement. Unfortunately, because they made these illiquid commitments prior to having their retirement income needs covered, they now find themselves in a very difficult position. They cannot afford to retire because of a lack of liquid investments to provide them with a consistent dependable income, nor can they liquidate their investments in the current severally depressed market. In addition, they are committed to annual tax reporting and increased tax preparer costs required for the illiquid assets.

If they had invested these same monies in their existing Free Market philosophy, they could have received market returns, appreciated in value, and it would always be liquid and available for them. In addition, they'd most likely have lower their taxes and tax preparation costs.

To invest for simplicity and peace of mind, stay liquid!

Avoid illiquid investments, as you cannot easily sell them to obtain a lump sum of money. If you have an illness and need some immediate medical expense money, it isn't available for you. Investing in illiquid assets limits your flexibility and options, as you cannot sell them quickly. That is what illiquid means, not available...or tied up! Usually when considering illiquid investments, Investors do not consider the worst-case scenario, the possible consequences of their decision. That scenario becomes readily apparent when there are problems.

> *The LORD... will... bring to light what is hidden in darkness*
> *and will expose the motives of men's hearts.*
>
> *– I Corinthians 4:5*

One type of illiquid investment to avoid is Limited Partnerships (LP), which have no or limited liquidity for many years, sometimes as long as 15 to 25 years. Jerry and I (Phyllis) have owned many LP's in our investment history, some have worked out just fine, but some have not. LP's are programs that bring a group of Investors together for a single purpose, i.e. to buy one or multiple properties, animals, strip malls, shipping containers, movies etc. The General Partner (GP) runs the program and has all the control. We have found that in some of the real estate programs we have invested in, the GP never even invested any of his own money into the program. Of course, you find that out too late!

The asset class category, risk level, that the various LP's fit into are already covered in the different multiple asset class categories. We repeat...there is no need or reason to create duplication between any asset classes already in your portfolio.

LP Investors also have to wait for their program's tax reporting k-1 form every spring before they can complete their taxes. Some GP's feel they are beyond the U.S. Securities and Exchange Commission (SEC) requirements! One GP did not send us a k-1 when it closed unexpectedly in 2003. The GP just decided not to communicate with us or our Investors. No communication, no reports until we repeatedly contacted the SEC. It was then in 2009 that the GP informed us that the program had been closed, back in 2003!

Along with staying away from LP's, we also suggest you avoid their sister programs, Real Estate Investment Trusts (REITS). Your money isn't tied up as long as Limited Partnerships since REITS are typically only five to seven-year programs. However, it is still an illiquid investment during those years, and you cannot withdraw your money unless you sell on the secondary market, which will greatly discount the value.

Here is an extreme illiquid situation. Learn more from our own experience, never invest in anything that eats or poops. You laugh, but just read and weep.

Jerry and I (Phyllis) invested in cattle and horses for a tax credit in the 1980s. Then in the government's infinite wisdom, they changed the tax credit laws and didn't "Grandfather" any of their changes. Wow, what a surprise! All our tax credits were backdated and voided. In addition, the owners of the cattle and horses did not put the Investors first, and more money was lost.

Offshore asset protection investing is another area we advise you to ignore, as we tried it for you. The investments are usually illiquid and not controlled by you. You must depend on an offshore banking or legal entity to fulfill your investment requests. Plus, there are high fees for this type of money management. Offshore investing is very difficult, as there is limited communication with the foreign entities, and you must rely on these foreign entities for compliance. These types of programs also create red flags for the IRS. You don't need or want the hassle, so avoid them. In fact, many offshore Investors are now voluntarily revealing their assets to the IRS, so they will not be escorted to prison cells.

If you really want simplicity, don't get involved in any investments that tie up your money or in investments you don't completely understand. We have already done that and endured the pain, so avoid our sufferings. We don't want you to have to go through the same difficult times we experienced, during your journey to financial freedom, contentment and success.

You can maintain contentment and peace of mind in your life through simplicity, keeping your investing lifestyle uncomplicated, and achieving your expectations. You can achieve them by capping your expenses, accumulating enough liquid wealth for your lifestyle needs, creating an appropriate inheritance for your children, and sharing the excess.

Please share this knowledge with your children, grandchildren and great-grandchildren. Spare them from experiencing these expensive investing problems.

I will open my mouth in parables, I will utter hidden things, things from of old-what we have heard and known, what our fathers have told us. We will not hide them from their children; we will tell the next generation the praiseworthy deeds of the LORD, his power, and the wonders he has done.
— Psalm 78: 2-4

Retail Mutual Funds

Retail mutual funds are mutual funds that the public can purchase through the no-load and commission broker dealers. Retail mutual funds have many problems. They will have a specific descriptive name, but that name does not necessarily mean the mutual fund invests according to its name. One large investment company has a global mutual fund that is more than 51% invested in the US. Yes, more domestic stock than foreign stock. No wonder Investors are confused!

All mutual funds are supposed to invest according to their stated investment objective. However, retail mutual funds have been fined by the SEC for various reasons, including being investing differently than their funds' stated investment objective. A retail mutual fund with a growth objective was investing in high-tech stock without asking the Investors to vote on changing the investment objective to aggressive and small company stock.

Other inappropriate and illegal activities have been the subject of SEC regulations against many mutual funds, including excessive trading—typically called turnover. Excessive turnover is called churning—which creates excessive expenses and excessive risks. We will discuss turnover later. Other mutual funds were fined millions by the SEC for late trading;

trading after the markets had closed. Some retail mutual funds were charged with fraud and fined by the SEC for an active money management trading strategy called market timing, moving into and out of market sectors as they heat up and cool off, which went against their prospectuses. Other funds failed to provide Investors with important information relating to their purchases of mutual fund shares, which means the Investors most likely did not receive their purchase discounts. We don't expect anyone to invest for free, however we do want mutual fund companies to follow the rules and not take advantage of Investors.

Every year since the early 1960's, many retail mutual have funds have disappeared, or died, and new funds were born. Have you ever had a mutual fund close or be combined with another fund? Why do you think a particular fund closed? There are many reasons for combining funds, some positive and beneficial to the Investor, however one major reason for closing mutual funds or combining funds is to lose a poor track record and identity, hiding yet another problem. Instead of correcting their investment faults, this technique folds them into another retail mutual fund, erasing their bad history and passing on the high expenses to the unsuspecting Investor.

All mutual funds have conflicts of interest. It doesn't matter if the mutual fund is a fee, no-load or commission mutual fund, someone is getting paid. *There is no free lunch!* A conflict of interest is when the person who is making the decision receives a benefit from the decision. Since conflicts are unavailable, make sure you understand them and can accept them as disclosed. Know your Investment Philosophy, use appropriate investment strategies for your belief, stay disciplined, and minimize your conflicts of interest as much as possible.

Funds that are managed in the Free Market globally diversified philosophy are institutional asset class mutual funds. Due to their funds' narrow objective and their disciple, they have not experienced the SEC fines or fraud problems: late trading, investment objectives not being followed, active trading, high turnover, and track record investing. The institutional mutual funds are named *true* to their objectives, such as domestic large company growth, international small company value, global 5 Yr. bonds, etc. Each mutual fund stays *true* to its name, as each category of stock or bond only fits into one level of risk, one asset class. If the asset class mutual fund name is domestic, it must hold only domestic stocks plus some cash. If the mutual fund's name says large company, it must contain stock of companies that qualify for the large company capitalization size, along with some cash so they can purchase more stock if necessary.

Stock mutual funds are either growth or value. Growth stock funds are for appreciation and value are distressed growth stock funds. Many times only the word "value" is included in the name, as growth is assumed by default, i.e.: "large international" means growth, "large international value" means value. Stock mutual funds can be many different categories or combination. The mutual funds asset class is determined by the fund's investment objective, as contained in the prospectus. We'll discuss various risk categories later.

Please be open to wisdom. Be aware and know there are many frauds and scandals you can avoid, just by being knowledgeable and accepting advice.

The way of a fool seems right to him,
but a wise man listens to advice.

— Proverbs 12:15

4

Is Retirement in Your Future?

The plans of the diligent lead to profit as surely as haste leads to poverty.

– Proverbs 21:5

Employer Retirement Plan Trap

Jill, an executive in a mid-sized company, is caught in an employee's investment trap. Her employer's investment committee chose a well-known very large annuity 401(k) plan and approved the employee investment options. You would think this committee should be knowledgeable, but instead the members seem to be living on an isolated island. They don't know what they don't know, and all the employees' future retirement lifestyles suffer!

The well-known very large company annuity 401(k) plan looks like it has no costs to the participants. You weren't born yesterday, you know *nothing is free* and *no one works for free*! Someone is being paid or is paying for these administrative costs, and sometimes someone is also paying to be part of the employee retirement plan options (called revenue sharing)! However, that isn't the worst problem.

After doing an analysis on this well-known large investment company's 401(k) annuity, we found most of the 20-plus asset

classes missing, so it also lacked prudent global diversification—
the most important ingredient in any portfolio. Sure, this large
401(k) annuity had 36 different mutual fund investment options
to choose from, but the long list of mutual funds all fit into only
four different asset class categories. That meant each of the 36
mutual funds is investing in the same stocks and bonds as
approximately nine other similar mutual funds! Just take a
moment to visualize a wooden ladder that you need to climb to
reach your home's 16-foot-high roof, your goal, but the ladder
only has four rungs spaced sporadically up the ladder's length.
Hard to accomplish your goal without 16-20 more rungs, spaced
evenly and continuously apart for you to climb.

This is also true with any investment. Jill's 401(k)'s
retirement ladder that she was given by her employer had only
four rungs to reach her goal, not the unique asset classes it
needed to be efficient and prudently diversified, as determined
by the Modern Portfolio Theory (MPT). Because the four unique
levels of investment choices are investing in various actively
managed mutual funds with similar objectives, they also created
a very expensive problem for Jill; they were duplicating multiple
stocks and bonds.

These employees are being duped with this abusive 401(k)
plan! The employer's Investment Committee must have thought
that diversification meant having many mutual fund options,
but they probably didn't realize that more "stuff" does not give
you prudent diversification. These investment options were all
similar, not different. When all those 36 mutual fund choices
are combined into only four unique asset classes, different levels
of risk, there is clearly duplication of investments, not the
desired prudent broad global diversification.

Would you rather invest in multiple unique global asset
classes or in only four and repeatedly trade the same stocks and
bonds?

> ***Investing in 16 to 20-plus unique asset classes in many free countries' stocks and bonds is truly broad global diversification.***

Another sad part of the story is that this same employer had changed its retirement plan a few years earlier from another very well known large abusive annuity 401(k) plan. They most likely took painfully expensive steps that lead to a worse place than where they already were. Yes, from the frying pan to the... fire!

We hope the Investment Committee didn't mean to hurt the employees and was convinced that the new plan was sure to succeed—yes, and hope springs eternal. However, the new retirement plan is just as bad or maybe even worse than the previous plan and possibly even worse for the employees, as they had to pay for all the buys and sells of moving the money. Nobody will ever know, as many of the expenses are hidden and the employees have not been taught how to achieve prudent broad diversification!

We are sure that if the employees knew the *truth*, they would be very upset and dissatisfied. Once employees read this book, they'll finally understand about prudent global diversification. We hope that knowledgeable concerned employees will take steps to correct employer retirement plans across the nation. Are you ready to change the world, starting with your own retirement plan's accounts? Take your new knowledge to work and help change your world!

When a mocker is punished, the simple gain wisdom; when a wise man is instructed, he gets knowledge.

– Proverbs 21:11

Advisors must always have the Investor's best interest as their first, second, and third concern. They must be guardians of their Investors. But in the real world, this is often compromised, as you have seen in the many recent financial scams and scandals reported by the media, and Jill's story. The job of the Advisor is to give the Investor the absolute best suitable investments at a favorable price, relative to available alternatives. This interest could compromise the revenue the Advisor, and his boss, the broker dealer, could realize, if they could move your money but don't. This is called a conflict of interest. A conflict of interest is created when the Investor is *not* put first and the advice is not objective!

Could it be that Jill's company's Advisor suggested the employer change annuity companies because he got a bigger commission with the second company? Unlike fiduciaries, Advisors from brokerage firms don't have to disclose if they have incentives to push one investment over another. In addition, Advisors in the retail financial industry are paid for investments sold, but not for advice, so they typically are in the "sales" mentality. Always *follow the money*!

Could it be that the very large well-known insurance company had its own proprietary "house mutual funds" in the 401(k)? Proprietary investments almost consistently underperform the market and are typically more expensive to the unsuspecting investor, especially employees who have no say in what company options they may have in their retirement plan! As mentioned in the previous chapter, stay away from retail proprietary "house" funds. Many times, Advisors' jobs depend less on giving advice and more on closing sales because the more money they bring in, the more they and their broker dealers earn. With profit making being a focus, many Advisors are encouraged by their brokerage company's highly paid analyst to push investments that are the "flavor of the month" and which bring in the most profit for the company. House funds are definitely not one of the best investments for Investors.

Our feelings are that brokerage firms, also known as broker dealers, should not be in the advisory business. Advisors who work through broker dealers should just tell Investors that they

work for a brokerage firm and s
disclose that they earn commissi(
conflict of interest. Investors car
they are more informed and have

Even if your retirement plan i:
plan, please read this section. The
follow the 1974 Employee Retii
(ERISA) guidelines. ERISA is ;
minimum standards of conduct f

industry. One of the guidelines states that every ERISA plan must have a fiduciary, someone who manages the employee benefit plan and its assets and is liable, held accountable and responsible, if there are any problems. Imposing a fiduciary requirement might have an impact on investment firms' profits, and that is just fine with us, as the Investors' accounts will be better protected.

One of the questions to ask every investment company that provides your retirement plan, including insurance companies, is "Are you an accountable ERISA fiduciary?" If they respond that they are the accountable type of ERISA fiduciary, get their answer written into the retirement plan's Investment Management Agreement. This level of fiduciary gives employers a great deal of coverage from liability, whereas other levels of fiduciary might not. Many 401(k) brochures say the investment company has fiduciary standards, which means your company has absolutely no protection from liability! It leaves all the fiduciary responsibilities to the employer. This is extremely essential. Employers, please only work with investment companies that will agree in writing to be your accountable fiduciary or co-fiduciary.

Fiduciary responsibilities cannot be eliminated, but they can be insulated with the support of not only a separate independent Advisor, but also a directed Trustee, and a Third Party Administrator (TPA). The TPA is the record keeper, sometimes an ERISA attorney. ERISA employer plans need all three separate entities, working to benefit their employee

se, if there is litigation, only the employer will
court, not the Investment Company or the
Advisor! Employers, don't wait until you are sued to
401(k) plan. Insulate your liabilities with a broadly
ified 401(k), explained further in Chapters 5 and 6.

*The eyes of the LORD are on the righteous and his ears are
attentive to their cry; the face of the LORD is against those
who do evil to cut off the memory of them from the earth.*
– Psalm 34:15-16

Every employer, including Jill's, needs to put its employees first. Employees depend on their employer to protect them and give them the very best available funds in their retirement plans. You should expect no less from your guardian Advisor. Employees do not deserve a retirement plan with problems: an annuity with hidden investment costs and surrender penalties, nor a front-loaded mutual fund plan with costs each time money is contributed, a back-loaded mutual fund plan with penalties or surrender fees, nor a C share mutual fund plan with larger costs—employees need the *best available plan*. Jill's company's Investment Committee—in fact, every employer—needs know what they don't know.

Sound investment strategies don't change with the economy, they are just like virtues, never changing.

Your portfolio should not need to change either. If anyone says you should change your portfolio when the market changes, they are not in harmony with the Free Market philosophy as this strategy remains constant in bull and bear markets.

Here is a quick review: Jill is paying too many fees and does not have any opportunity for prudent diversification in the limited 401(k) asset class options. It is almost impossible for her to reach his goals and dreams within his retirement account, as

78

she has a retirement ladder with only four rungs, lack of broad global diversification, no correlation, no plan for rebalancing, plus high hidden expenses. Jill's retirement account is not growing like she and her family need it to be in order to obtain their retirement goals. This will continue as long as the company's Investment Committee does not follow the Prudent Investor Rule of 1994, suggested that all ERISA plans follow. The Prudent Investor Rule, drafted by the National Conference of Commissioners on Uniform State Laws and approved and recommended by it for enactment in all the states in 1994, and it was approved by the American Bar Association in 1995. The Prudent Investor Rule actually mentions the Modern Portfolio as an example as to how ERISA plans need to offer globally diversified options. However, most corporate investment committees are not listening. Do you think there is some bottom line profit, revenue sharing, or ego problems involved here? Could the investment committee really be so arrogant, complacent, shortsighted, and greedy, or is it truly ignorant of the Uniform Prudent Investor Act and lacks knowledge of what prudent diversification looks like?

Jill's employer's Investment Committee will hopefully follow the Prudent Investor Rule once the 401(k) plan does not pass their Department of Labor (DOL) audit and their employer is charged a hefty fine. Possibly then they'll look for a much broader diversified strategy, which takes advantage of the academic Nobel Prize winning Modern Portfolio, and if properly designed and rebalanced quarterly, should pass a DOL audit.

If you do not have an ERISA retirement plan at work, don't assume your retirement plan does not have many of the same problems. If you have any type of retirement plan at work, ERISA or not, and it does not offer prudent diversification (at least 16 – 20 different risk levels of asset classes) you also most likely have inadequate diversification of investment options, higher risk, no correlation, no rebalancing, and larger costs.

Now that you know and have knowledge of potential

problems, please take action. We'll show you how in the "Pass It Along" section, after the Employer Questions.

Get wisdom, get understanding; do not forget my words or swerve from them. Do not forsake wisdom, and she will protect you; love her, and she will watch over you. Wisdom is supreme; therefore get wisdom.

Though it cost all you have, get understanding. Esteem her, and she will exalt you; embrace her, and she will honor you. She will set a garland of grace on your head and present you with a crown of splendor. Hold on to instruction, do not let it go; guard it well, for it is your life.

— Proverbs 4:5-9, 13

Questions for Retirement Plan Employers

1. ERISA Plans:
   a. ERISA Plan Fiduciaries are personally liable for breaches of fiduciary standards. How much wealth could you lose if your plan's audit fails?
   b. Has the Department of Labor conducted an audit on your plan? If so, what were the results?
2. How many unique asset classes does your plan offer?
3. What is the turnover rate of each mutual fund in your plan?
4. How do you specifically measure the amount of risk and volatility in your plan or any of the fund choices?
5. Do you have a clear-cut method for measuring the success or failure of your plan?
6. How do your plan participants get access to independent professional investment advice in order to design their own portfolios with the plan?
7. Do your plan participants complain about their returns? Would you have less employee retention problems if you offered a better plan?
8. What is the ongoing education process that you use to help your plan participants be more educated and knowledgeable

regarding their retirement? Is the education also available on the Internet?

Do you see a man skilled in his work? He will serve before kings; He will not serve before obscure men.

– Proverbs 22:29

Pass it Along

Employees, if your retirement plan at work (not only 401(k) and other ERISA plans, but also 403b, Tax Sheltered Annuity, 403b7, Profit Sharing, SIMPLE IRA Plan, SARSEP, SEP, etc.) doesn't offer the stress-free Four-Step Investing Process, what are you *committed* to doing?

You can change your world if you stand up and challenge the status quo. ERISA plan employees can save their company a lot of future DOL audit stress, money, and potential regulatory problems, especially if your company avoids a failed audit. Every employee can potentially save other employees a lot of hidden fees, inadequate returns, and years of surrender charges by speaking up. You might even be voted the most popular employee in your company. Are you ready to step up and make a difference for the good of all your peers at work?

Let us therefore make every effort to do what leads to peace and to mutual edification.

– Romans 14:19

If your answer is "No" what do you have to lose? Are you afraid? Fear freezes many well-deserved informed and well-intentioned behaviors and actions. You may already have an inadequate retirement plan with poor returns, so you might be struggling to achieve your retirement goal. Your efforts can only improve your retirement plan, as your employer most likely also wants happy employees, so please reconsider.

If your answer is "Yes" give this book to your boss, Employee Benefits Dept., or employer's Investment Committee, with all your highlighted and underlined notes. Congratulations for being proactive! Just do what's right; yes... it is a virtue!

Ask your Boss/Investment Committee/Employee Benefits Director to read this chapter and chapter seven. Your employer must be informed! People at the helm of your company are typically looking for better and cheaper ways to run the company.

If they take action, you'll be thanked in the beginning when their liability is moved to a third-party fiduciary, and then you'll be thanked again when the company passes its DOL audit. You might even get your very own, well-deserved parking space!

The righteous cry out, and the LORD hears them;
he delivers them from all their troubles.

– Psalm 34:17

Your Retirement Lifestyle

Jake was a highly successful upper-level manager in the automotive business. He was the manager of a very large division and well respected. His whole identity and self-worth was related to his position at work. Jake worked too long, too much, had no outside interests and took very few vacations. He and his wife Lynn didn't have children, so their whole focus was on work and themselves. They were estranged from their relatives, as they never had time for vacations nor did they attend family reunions. Lynn was proud of her beautiful home, her antique car, and her "stuff." Jake was proud of his position at work. However, his division was reorganized, and he was involuntarily retired. Jake had no plans for what he was going to do during his retirement, so he did just that... nothing. Once retired, Jake was lonely and saw no reason to get out of bed in the morning. He began drinking at night, then at noon, and eventually he drank immediately upon rising in the morning.

Jake died within six months of retirement of alcoholism, loneliness and depression. Lynn is now alone in her beautiful home with her beautiful furniture, glorious clothes, fancy cars, and no friends. Is that the kind of life you want when you retire? We hope not, so let's get some ideas flowing!

Are you planning to retire some day? Awesome! Now make sure it happens the way you want it to. Take a moment to visualize what you'll be doing after your retirement party. Statistics show that most Investors live quite a long time after their retirement party. Women especially, plan to live at least to the age of 90! Ladies, how old was your mother when she passed to her eternal glory? A woman must plan to live at least seven years longer than her mother. Some of you need to plan to live for a century. Be thankful for your great genes! What do you want to do for the second half of your life? What lifestyle will make you content? Remember, earthly possessions will stay here when you die, as you take nothing tangible to eternity.

> *But godliness with contentment is a great gain. For we brought nothing into the world, and we can take nothing out of it. But if we have food and clothing, we will be content with that.*
>
> *– I Timothy 6:6-8*

Quickly draw a sketch of what your future retirement looks like. There is only one rule, you must dream big! What do you really want to do when you retire? Yes, think about the very *best* retirement you can imagine! Are you sailing, traveling, reading books, gardening, moving to a different home, spending more time with family, volunteering, living in the same home you are in now, etc.? Everyone's picture will be different, as we are all unique with unique dreams. Your retirement preparation will also be unique.

You can change your retirement "dream" picture every day if you like, but start dreaming and figuring out what you want to do during retirement. Or you might dream about not fully retiring, but just changing careers—the choice is yours! You must look at your future retirement head on and face reality. Every day you are getting older, and the time you have left on earth is getting shorter. Your best asset is your health, so take good care of yourself and use your time wisely.

Are you married? If so, both spouses have dreams and both must be heard. If our Investors are married, we request both spouses attend our Coaching appointments so we hear all the dreams, not just a portion.

When meeting with one middle-aged couple, the uninterested wife refused to attend. She was cordial and greeted us when we entered their home, but then decided she wasn't interested in talking about money or retirement, so excused herself and read a magazine in another room.

Listen to us, *ladies you matter!* Money is *not* a taboo or bedroom topic. Your spouse cannot express your dreams as well as you can. Your Advisors don't know your dreams and desires unless you voice them. Sure, goals can always be changed, they are flexible, so don't be afraid to voice your current feelings and desires, and then change them as needed. Start talking, thinking, dreaming and sharing your retirement dreams! Talk to your spouse, your children, and your friends—discover and be aware of your own feelings. God will direct your path!

> *Ladies, you must be involved in all the planning for your family, including retirement planning.*

Statistically the female will outlive her spouse; therefore, women are likely the ones who are going to benefit the *most* from this planning. It is very important that your dreams and wishes be known, discussed, and planned for, so you will have no regrets in the future. In addition, once you become single again, and reality sets in, you will need to finally face the music and do what you avoided before, so *let's get this done now!* You are younger today than tomorrow, and tomorrow might never come, so keep progressing in this book, move forward, keep reading and keep an open mind.

For many Investors, their retirement goal is total financial freedom with a certain income level. The income goal for one Investor might be considered excess income by another. The amount you need is not what matters, as the basics are the same. Determine what amount of income you need per year to fulfill your dreams and invest in order to cover your gap, i.e. the income needed but not yet covered by other retirement income. Once you know the amount of income you need over and above any other retirement income, then calculate withdrawing up to an annual maximum of 4-5% from your investments, taking just enough to cover your lifestyle gap. If you find that you do not have enough investments to cover your gap with only a 4-5% distribution per year, now is the time to make some changes. Invest more or move out of income type of investing into growth investments with a potential higher rate of return. You can do one or both: alter your current lifestyle expenses or invest for more growth.

Ask your Coach to do a Retirement Cash Flow Analysis so you can make sure you are climbing the right retirement ladder. Do not depend on winning the lottery or receiving an inheritance to fulfill your retirement income needs. That is *not* a retirement plan! You are responsible for providing for your family and loved ones, so the income gap analysis is very important. We want you content during your golden years.

If anyone does not provide for his relatives, and especially for his immediate family, he has denied the faith and is worse than an unbeliever

— I Timothy 5:8

Key Retirement Plan Points

1. Know investing basics.

There are two types of liquid investments, debt (produces interest or income) and equity (growth for appreciation).

a. Debt: Saving is *not* investing! Saving in money market accounts, Savings Accounts, Certificates of Deposit (CD), Tax-free Municipal Bonds, and similar instruments is accumulating money in debt instruments that have dividends or interest and minimal market risk. However, they do have huge inflation risks, as many years they don't earn enough to offset inflation, so over time, you'll most likely be losing purchasing power. Saving is for emergencies and for short-term goals, a goal that will use the money within three years. Your emergency account of two to three months living expenses is most likely in a debt or income-producing instrument like a CD or savings account at the Credit Union or bank. This is not the place to invest for your future.

b. Equity: Equity investing has historically been the best wealth creation tool. Investing is a long-term strategy and the best strategy is with equities, through the ownership of domestic and international company shares, which means you expect some growth. Growth means you are investing for appreciation, an increase of value, and for your future. Growth instruments are typically ownership vehicles such as: stocks, growth mutual funds, annuities, and real estate. Growth investments hopefully become more valuable—like your home. You hope over the years that your home appreciates in value, so when you sell, you want to sell it for more than you paid for it, a long-term gain. Get excited about investing! Your children might catch your excitement and follow your lead.

> *Train child in the way he should go,*
> *and when he is old he will not turn from it.*
>
> *—Proverbs 22:6*

c. Inflation: In order to keep bringing home the same amount of groceries each year, you must keep up with inflation. Inflation never retires, so you must always get returns that are larger than it, or you'll lose purchasing power. It is advisable to have a portion of your portfolio always in growth investments, yes...stock. The easiest way to invest in stock is to invest in growth mutual funds. Stocks are many times higher risk than bonds, debt investments, but investing in a broadly correlated (various amounts of different levels of risk that react dissimilar in the market) global stock portfolio, as we'll explain in the following chapters, reduces that risk. Only through ownership, not debt, can your investments appreciate and stay ahead of inflation. What percentage of your portfolio should be stock? That depends on your comfort with risk and your understanding of how risk is reduced through diversification. The rule of thumb is: the longer you can wait to use your investments, the higher the risk you can take and the more consistently you'll outpace inflation. If you desire to be wealthy, you must invest in assets with risk.

d. Plan Ahead *Now*: Providing for your old age is Biblical. Make sure you are investing appropriately for your risk tolerance and unique goals. Yes, you need money for today, but don't neglect investing in your future lifestyle. Start with at least $100 a month, then increase it every year. The younger you start, the less it costs to cover your future needs. It's cheaper now than it will ever be in the future because of *compounding and time are your friends!*

> *In the house of the wise are stores of choice food and oil, but a foolish man devours all he has.*
>
> *— Proverbs 21:20*

e. Beneficiaries: Providing an inheritance for your family is also Biblical. Make sure your beneficiary choices are up to date. If you have experienced a life-changing event, such as marriage or divorce, or a new child, immediately checking and changing your current beneficiaries is extremely important.

> *A good man leaves an inheritance for his children's children...*
>
> *— Proverbs 13:22*

2. Know your employer's retirement plan.

a. Do not invest in any annuities within any of your employer's tax-deferred retirement plans, such as: SIMPLE IRA, 403b, TSA, 401(k), Simplified Employee Pension, SARSEP, or 501c3. These are IRS plans created to be tax-deferred, so it makes absolutely no sense to invest in a tax-deferred investment within a tax-deferred IRS plan. Did you notice that the same words "tax-deferred" were just used twice? Even the IRS is upset, as many insurance companies have received IRS penalties for promoting annuities in retirement plans. Invest in taxable investments within your retirement plan...then you receive the real tax-deferred benefits!

b. Many university and medical hospitals have stifling retirement plans with fixed and variable annuities. The fixed annuity might have a 10% liquidity feature, meaning you may only take 10% out per year to use or move to a better growth investment. The expensive active managed variable annuity portion of this plan has a surrender charge, but eventually that goes away. We urge you not to get caught up in these types of retirement programs, especially if there is no matching by your employer. If you already are in one like this, start moving your 10% fixed annuity at once to another investment, such as a no-load mutual fund that has no connection with an annuity; therefore, you could have no surrender fees or penalties. Most universities and teaching hospitals also have that type of option, but often it isn't announced. You *must ask* for it. Once retired, you are no longer committed to these inappropriate investments; you can then move 100% to the Free Market philosophy.

c. As we mentioned earlier, if your employer's ERISA plan at work only has a tax-deferred annuity option, do yourself and your friends at work a favor and *please speak up*! Contact your employer's benefits department and tell them you need better taxable options in your tax-deferred retirement plan. It is the law. Your employer's benefits department needs to follow the Uniform Prudent Investor Act, which ERISA plans are required to follow. It states that the appropriate strategy for diversification is the Modern Portfolio Theory (MPT), which is one of the components of the efficient market philosophy.

d. If your employer doesn't offer funds that follow the efficient market philosophy as one of your investment options, your Free Market Coach can help. He'll advise you how to invest using your existing employer's retirement plan options to get as close as possible to the MPT broad global diversification strategy and the Three Factor Model. Ask your Coach to analyze your retirement plan and help you with the a retirement plan management program.

e. If your employer's retirement plan offers a Roth 401(k) option for your contributions, choose this option instead of the tax-deferred 401(k). The Roth plan uses after-tax dollars, so you'll pay your taxes on those dollars before they are invested. It is better to pay taxes on your investment "seed" and not your investment "harvest." Your employer's match, if any, will be in the typical tax-deferred 401(k), so you'll have to pay taxes on those amounts when you retire and take them as distributions—or better yet, convert them to your Roth as soon as possible. Don't count on being on a lower income tax rate after your retirement. This doesn't happen for many retirees.

f. If there is no employer match in your employer's retirement plan, just focus on maxing out your Roth—see #3 below. The ideal situation is to do enough in your employer's plan to get the maximum free money, plus every year also max out your Free Market Roth outside your employer's retirement plan.

g. Only invest in your employer's stock if you have to. Remember Enron? Your paycheck comes from this company, so it is best to diversify your retirement investments into the broad global market. If your employer contributes its own stock in its 401(k), take it. However, as soon as you are able liquidate the stock and move your monies into broad global diversification, using other investment options within your 401(k). You'll lower your risks.

h. Each time you change jobs and when you retire, move your retirement plan account immediately into your Free Market IRA or Roth for the broadest diversification, lowest risk, and least costs. The sooner you move these funds, the sooner you can experience peace of mind.

Turn from evil and do good;
seek peace and pursue it.

— Psalm 34:14

3. Fund your Roth and your spouse's Roth every year!

Your Roth is the absolute *best retirement plan* the government has ever given you to help you gain your financial freedom. It can make your retirement lifestyle abundant and completely independence from needing any government entitlement programs. The Roth grows *tax-free* forever, so please don't fund it with any retail/commercial tax-deferred investment. The costs of retail investments are often too high, and Investors lose potential growth. It is difficult to cover all the active money managers' turnover costs. Princeton University's Economics Professor Malkiel concurs in his book *A Random Walk Down Wall Street,* "active managers charge substantial investment fees, and their buying and selling of securities in their attempt to beat the market generates significant transaction costs." Please check the Book & DVD List.

Plan well so you are truly financially free. The Roth can be taken away from us anytime by legislation, so invest the maximum contribution allowed every year into the Free Market philosophy.

Make it your ambition to lead a quiet life, to mind your own business and to work with your hands, just as we told you, so that your daily life may win the respect of outsiders and so that you will not be dependent on anybody.
– I Thessalonians 4:11-12

4. The best time to invest for retirement is now!

The easiest way to save is with automatic bank withdrawals. Automatically invest at least 15% to 20% of your gross paycheck, no matter what the market is doing. This technique is called "Dollar Cost Averaging," explained in the next section. To be a successful Investor, consider *putting your future first*—yes, even before the current bills are paid. If you focus on your goals, your lifestyle will adjust as you consistently invest. It is about self-preservation and self-interest, this is not selfishness. Taking care of yourself and your family should always be your priority.

5. Do you need more retirement money because your 401(k) or Roth isn't enough?

Open up a taxable personal account using the Free Market philosophy and contribute monthly, holding it for the long term, preferably your lifetime. Invest for growth, as growth portfolios receive very few dividends and have greater potential for giving you more appreciation value, however growth investments will have higher risks than bond investments. Appreciation however is taxed at the tax advantaged long-term capital gains rate, typically a lower tax rate than your income tax rate. If your account registration is not a Revocable Living Trust account or joint account, make sure you make it a payable on death (POD) account registration, so it can avoid probate.

6. Is your income too large to contribute to a Roth?

If so, open up a Non-Deductible (ND) IRA for both spouses and contribute the maximum to it. You'll not claim the contributions on your 1040 as every January you can convert your ND IRA to your Roth, and then you'll only pay taxes on the gain.

Go to the ant, you sluggard; consider its ways and be wise!
It has no commander, no overseer or ruler, yet it stores its
provisions in summer and gathers its food at harvest.
— Proverbs 6:6-8

Dollar Cost Averaging

Rosemary, a schoolteacher, started Dollar Cost Averaging in 1987. One day she called to thank us for teaching our financial education classes at the local college and encouraging her to make some investing changes. Rosemary was retiring and wanted us to know that without her attending the classes and hearing about how to invest, she wouldn't have been able to retire early. She was very happy she had followed our advice to put money into her 403b every paycheck from the time she attended our classes until her retirement. Without saving every payday (Dollar Cost Averaging) Rosemary wouldn't have been able to retire when she wanted and with as healthy a nest egg.

We love to hear from our students. Dollar Cost Averaging is buying a certain amount of mutual fund shares in all market cycles—when the market is moving down as well as when the market is moving up. This technique of putting the same amount of money into the market at regular intervals means you'll be investing some money when stocks are high, but also when the market is at its lowest. When you make an investment into your mutual fund account, your money buys shares of your mutual fund at the market's ending value for that day. If at the end of the next day the share value goes down, you still own the same number of shares. When you again deposit the same amount of money into your mutual fund while the market is still down, you buy more shares than you did earlier at the higher price, as they are purchased at a lower price, or *on sale*, so that lowers your average costs. When the market goes back up, the value of the shares you bought for less (*sale* shares) will also appreciate with your other shares, but you'll have *more* shares appreciating to a higher value.

Remember, you are always "in the market", and Dollar Cost Averaging has risks, it does not insure profit or protect against loss.

Buying: Assume the first shares you purchased in your mutual fund cost $1.00 per share on Payday #1. Your deposit of $10 will purchase 10 shares of the mutual fund (shares are also called units).

Payday #2 you have another $10 to deposit, but the market has gone down, so now the shares in the mutual fund have a value of $.50 per share (half the earlier price). Your $10 deposit will now buy 20 shares, double what you purchased on Payday #1. That's a great discount!

You now own 30 shares, so when the market goes back up, and it eventually will, your mutual fund share value will appreciate more because you bought shares at the depressed (*sale*) price, plus you now have more shares that get to appreciate with the market!

Don't you love paying less for items on *sale*? The market is *"on sale"* when share values go down. Most women love discounts! Would you rather buy shares at $.50 or wait until the shares go back to $1? Keep adding money every payday and you too will eventually thank us. When your favorite groceries are *on sale*, you purchase extra because you get more for your hard-earned money, but why don't you do the same when the market is "*on sale*"? It's the same concept.

The sad reality is that the typical average Investor thinks and behaves just the opposite. Research shows that investors hurt themselves, as they buy at market highs and sell at market lows.

Selling: Would you rather sell your shares for $.50 or $1? Selling at a higher price than what you bought them for is the #1 investment rule—Buy Low, Sell High. This happens when your money manager quarterly rebalances your accounts by selling off the excess gain (Sell High), the amount over each asset's target amount and applies it to the asset classes that have moved below their targets (Buy Low). We'll talk more about rebalancing later.

Maintaining: If you just hold but are unable to add to your accounts, you'll continue to own the same number of shares. When the market goes down, your share value will be less, this is called a "paper loss" because you have not actually sold any shares. It isn't a "realized loss," it is only a temporary loss on paper. The history of investing shows us that the market has always recovered, sometimes after very prolonged periods of down markets and in some cases investors had to wait years before getting even. However, when it does rebound, it typically rebounds quickly and higher than where it was before the downturn. Just be patient and stay in the market.

Time: *Time is your best friend!* The earlier you start systematically investing, the better! Do not be in a rush to become wealthy, just stay disciplined and *stay committed.* Be patient and keep investing every payday, and your wealth will grow over time. Obey the rules of investing and don't take on risks beyond what is necessary! Read Proverbs 28:20-22.

If they obey and serve him, they will spend the rest of their days in prosperity and their years in contentment. But if they do not listen, they will perish by the sword and die without knowledge.

— Job 36:11-12

Celebrate When the Market Goes Down!

Let's review some of the information you just learned. Free Market Investors no longer worry when markets go down because they know:

1. You can buy shares of asset class mutual funds at very low prices and receive more shares—the market truly is *on sale*! Just think discounts...you can change your financial future, if you take advantage of market *sales*.

2. Of course, there is no guarantee, but history shows that higher market returns always follow soft markets, also called "bear", and over time, a down market will just be another historical blip on a market growth continuum.

3. It is a great time to get down to the basics, re-evaluate your goals, and your risk tolerance. If you can't sleep during market downturns, consider transferring to less growth (less stock) and more interest (more bonds), but not *until* your portfolio recoups. Change your portfolio slowly, as you have time working for you. After the blip, you'll need to reassess the amount of risk you are willing to take in your portfolio.

4. The media is showing their real colors... selling fear of the future instead of educating investors. The media is *not* your friend. Remember, they need to sell something, such as newspapers, TV time, magazines, radio ads, etc. *Always follow the money!* Seek the *truth* in whatever you hear and read!

5. The perfect time to convert your IRA to your Roth is when its value is discounted, temporarily low. When your account value is down, there is less to convert, therefore, you'll pay

less tax next April—tax day! This allows the value to rebound once in the Roth!

6. If your annuity value is "below its cost basis" (cost of investing), consider moving your money from the annuity to a growth portfolio that uses the Free Market philosophy. Your future distributions will no longer be taxed according to income tax rates, as the annuity's gains are taxed, but instead only be taxed at long-term growth rates.

7. According to the Bull and Bear Markets Report by CRSP (1/1/1926–8/1/208) and Bloomberg (9/1/2008-3/31/2010) the average duration of a "down" bear market from 1/1/1926 – 3/31/2010 is 220 days. The longer the bear market lasts, the closer you are to the next up market—also called a bull market. Stay invested so you don't miss out on the market movements.

8. Keep continually investing, buying more discounted shares, cheaper! On the other side of the sell trades—from all the people liquidating their portfolios due to their irrational fear—are Investors who want to buy the market when it is *"on sale"*. Keep buying those discounted shares!

9. Unless you sell your holdings, your losses are only on paper. When you sell at a low market period, you have locked in your losses. You'll miss the upturn in the market without those monies in the market, as it is hard to know when to get back in. Market recoveries, after prolonged downturns, tend to come in quick sudden bursts. To capture those recoveries, just stay disciplined, stay the course. Be committed to your Investment Philosophy beliefs and accumulation plan.

10. The efficient market philosophy invests in the broad global market: 12,000-plus unique stocks and bonds from 40 plus different free countries within 20-plus institutional asset allocation funds. We have not found anyone better diversified these Investors.

11. Investors who "Dollar Cost Average" by continually adding to their investments will come out the biggest winners. Just keep focusing on the long term, stay globally diversified, and keep your money in the market. *Don't follow the crowd!* Once diversified in the stress-free philosophy, resist the urge to change anything. You do not have to make changes when the market changes. Stay *true* to your beliefs.

12. Micropal, a global leader in providing independent information on mutual funds, did a study of the average annual returns for a series of series of hypothetical $1,000 investments in the stock market, as represented by the S&P 500 Index, made on the best day and worst day each year, 1/1/84-12/31/08. The difference between the Investor who invested on the worst market day of each year vs. the Investor who invested on the best market day of each year was only 1.97%. Therefore, the best time to invest is when you have the money. Don't wait for the best time to invest. Past performance doesn't predict future performance.

> ### *The best time to invest is yesterday, today, tomorrow, and now!*

---

13. Historically, the Free Market philosophy is a WIN-WIN-WIN game, however no one can guarantee the future, as the past is not predictive of the future. Visualize being in a large boat with many other Investors, riding the ocean waves, called the market. The Investors in the boat who are investing the same are getting similar returns, as no one is better diversified, outperforming anyone else, nor is anyone paying more costs than any other Investor. We are in this all together. It isn't about some winning and others losing, we are all winners. It is an up and down ride on the market cycle waves, without worrying if we'll get better or worse returns than other Investors. When the waves are at their

lowest—the market is on *sale*—and it is a great time to buy. When the waves are highest, it is the best time to sell. Buy low, sell high! Selling is done very infrequently, and when it is done, it is done through rebalancing, which we'll explain in Chapters 5 and 6.

14. Compounding is your buddy! Your money can earn dividends, which are reinvested, appreciate, and earn more dividends building value. Over time, your money makes more money for you. Keep building up your shares and you'll be rewarded in greater ways than you image.

God's voice thunders on marvelous ways; he does great things beyond our understanding.

– Job 37:5

Test Drive Your Retirement Dreams

Karl and Jenny retired and sold their home to move to a warmer climate. They were looking forward to full-time fishing, golfing and gardening, as their new southern home was near a lake and on a golf course. Two years after their move, they called us to help them figure out how to repurchase their previous home, the same home they had left behind in southeast Michigan. They wanted to move back. They missed their children and grandchildren and decided that family was more important to them than year-round warm weather, golfing, fishing, and gardening. Unfortunately, they could not buy back their old home, so they bought a different home in their previous town but still near their family. They also bought a timeshare in their favorite vacation location, where they liked to golf and fish during Michigan's cold winter months.

This was a very expensive mistake for Karl and Jenny. Selling your home and moving to a new location without trying out your new lifestyle first can bring retirees back home, unhappy with their chosen retirement lifestyle decisions. Take time to make your retirement decisions and try them out before making large changes. Maybe your heart really doesn't want to say "good bye" to your previous life.

Retirement is about more than your finances, it is also about your lifestyle and happiness. Take advantage of the years before your retirement. Try living on your retirement income and test drive your dreams to make sure they are realistic. Sometimes perception is not reality. Visit the location(s) where you might like to retire for an extended time and experience the lifestyle you think you might enjoy. You might find out that your dream, once experienced, is not exactly what you truly desire. This is a very inexpensive way to avoid a potential very expensive mistake!

In his heart a man plans his course,
but the LORD determines his steps.
— Proverbs 16:9

Freedom from Social Security

Emily is 63 and scared. She is frustrated about the possibility of Social Security changing. Having had a terrible experience with the returns on her employer's 401(k) retirement plan, she now sees more potential trouble ahead for her retirement lifestyle. Retiring during a down market, Emily depended completely on her 401(k) investments for her retirement income, but the retail mutual funds her retirement plan offered never rebounded after the last crash. Her retirement income from her depressed investments would not cover her bills. Emily worked for a large professional firm for 27 years and depended on her bosses and co-workers to show her how she should invest. Her loyalty hurt her.

Sadly, their advice and her plan failed her, as expensive mutual funds with minimal diversification and with duplication of investments were her only investment options. Now Emily is more concerned, as her "emergency money," as she previously called her Social Security check, has turned into her "mandatory money." She is now required to depend on her Social Security check to supplement her 401(k) income just to maintain her retirement lifestyle.

Are you striving to become financially independent, free from any entitlement programs? If so, do not anticipate using Social Security in your Retirement Cash Flow Analysis. Yes, it might be there, but to be financially independent and enjoy financial freedom, you need to control your own retirement income and not depend on the government for any paycheck. That's right, it is better to plan on *no* money from Uncle Sam.

Make sure you pass this knowledge on to your heirs. Help them learn financial self-sufficiency, by not depending on any entitlement programs, and encouraging personal responsibility and accountability. After all, who can depend on Social Security, which according to The Heritage Center for Data Analysis as quoted by William Beach Jan. 15, 1998 in *Social Security's Rate of Return*, has appreciated approximately 1.2% in real rates of return since your money was contributed? Your own investments can do much better than that. In addition, the more financially free you are, the easier it is for you to volunteer more time to your favorite ministries and give more lifetime gifts to your heirs. The enviable life!

Not only share your knowledge but also share your time, care, and wealth with your heirs while you are alive.

You might learn a lot about your heirs, how they handle money, and if they appreciate your support and mentoring now while you are alive. You don't have to give them money. Your gifts can be your time, teaching them how to make things, cooking, sewing, building, heirlooms, favorite items, collections, homemade items, tuition, etc. Then watch carefully what they do with your gifts. It'll tell you if they are appreciative and knowledgeable about money, and if they'll be able to handle a larger inheritance. If disappointed, you hopefully have time to educate them to become more responsible, or you can change your inheritance plans.

Dale and Julie are community workers and don't have a large retirement account; however, their inheritance to their children is paying for their children's college education. This is an excellent inheritance, giving their children the foundation for becoming self-sufficient and financially successful in life. An inheritance does not need to be a large amount of cash or "stuff". In the Old Testament, the inheritance passed down to the next generation was typically land and animals and not given equally to each heir. None of your heirs are the same, so don't assume their inheritances should also be the same. A large sum of money can be helpful or hurtful. Be careful you do not hurt your heirs. Read: Job 42:15 and Proverbs 13:22.

Help your heirs by following these Social Security Freedom Steps and by starting a Free Market Roth for each of them—see Step #5 in the next section.

So then men ought to regard us as servants of Christ and as those entrusted with the secret things of God.
Now it is required that those who have been given a trust must prove faithful.
— I Corinthians 4:1-2

Repetition is Good for the Smartest of Minds

Follow these steps and share this knowledge with your loved ones. Help them *avoid* relying on Social Security at retirement. Sure there is some repetition, and as we have said, repetition is good for even the smartest of minds.

Step #1: Stop losing money!

Confirm that your employer's tax-deferred retirement plan offers *true* asset class mutual fund options. These inexpensive institutional asset class mutual funds give Investors prudent global diversification, eliminate a lot of stock and bond duplication, and avoid insurance mortality risk costs, which are expensive additional annuity costs. Investors with prudently diversified investments can receive market returns with less risk, less volatility, and less expense—better and cheaper! If you don't have globally diversified 401(k) investment options, and you do not receive any employer match, *stop* contributing to your 401(k) and therefore, stop putting more good money into a poorly diversified plan. Contribute the maximum into your Free Market Roth instead. If you do have an employer matching program in your under diversified 401(k), invest only enough to qualify for the maximum free money match and put the rest of your retirement savings into your Roth.

Step #2: Ask your employer to offer the Roth 401(k).

If you only have the tax-deferred 401(k) retirement plan at work, ask your employer to add the Roth 401(k) option to your existing 401(k) plan. Once the Roth 401(k) is offered, put 100% of your employee contributions into the Roth after tax option and currently the employer will only match into the 401(k)'s traditional pre-tax tax-deferred option. If the Roth 401(k) isn't offered, open your own Free Market Roth and invest the maximum allowed each and every year you are eligible. The Roth is *Uncle Sam's best-kept secret,* and it is time to take this secret out of the retirement plan closet. Check with your Coach or your Roth plan sponsor as to what the Roth's maximum contribution amount is each year and what the income ceilings are, as the contribution amounts frequently change and maximum contributions are meant to keep up with inflation. Hopefully, the Roth's maximum contribution amounts continue to increase.

Step #3: Put your retirement goal first!

Yes, you must put your retirement needs first. You aren't being selfish. You must be proactive and act with self-interest. The easiest way to accumulate wealth for all your goals, including retirement, is by compounding with Dollar Cost Averaging. Have your money invested each time you get paid, or at least once a month, directly from payroll or your checking account. Whether the market is up or down, it is the right time to invest—just keep contributing. Don't worry about what you hear in the media...it's mostly noise. *Just keep investing.*

If you don't take care of yourself, who will? We want you to be financially healthy, so take action and put yourself first. You have taken care of everyone else until now, so let's take care of the person in the mirror—yes, *you*!

Step #4: Convert your tax-deferred retirement plans.

If you believe tax rates will be going up, consider converting your retirement plans into your Roth before your 70th birthday. By paying your tax early, 100% of any future appreciation is yours income tax-free, forever, once your Roth is 5 years old! We call this plan: "short-term pain" (pay income taxes now) for "long-term gain" (never pay tax again on these monies). It is best if you can time your conversions with lower taxable income years. The younger you are when you convert (IRA, 401(k), SEP, SARSEP, SIMPLE IRA, Profit Sharing), the greater the tax-free appreciation benefits. Converted IRA money also eliminates future IRA Required Minimum Distributions (RMD). Think, tax elimination!

In addition, you actually gain more control. Converting to the Roth allows you to pass this *tax-free* Roth to your heirs *tax-free* if you don't deplete your Roth account before you graduate to your eternal glory. This is probably the most important benefit of IRA conversions into a Roth.

Step #5: Open up Roths for all your younger family members ASAP!

Help your family and change their lives forever. The younger your family members, the more you can help them. The Roth has great benefits! First, as mentioned before, it grows *tax-free* forever and amounts you don't spend go to your heirs income *tax-free*! The IRS does not enjoy a piece of your retirement pie, as it does with all tax-deferred retirement plans. Stop investing for the IRS!

Another benefit is that early withdrawals are allowed for higher education tuition and first home purchases. A definite WIN-WIN-WIN for Roth Investors! The Investor wins, the Coach wins as he now has a happy Investor, and an heir or ministry also wins! Moreover, helping your heirs with their Roths will allow you to educate them on the *truths* of investing and how important it is to be globally diversified. Personal experience with Free Markets is a great reality experience.

The need for a Social Security check can be eliminated for young Investors. Everyone, including pre-teens, who plans to eventually retire, needs to learn the *truths* of investing, not by playing the stock market game taught in most schools. The Free Market Portfolio Theory needs to be taught in all middle schools and high schools. If you have any influence in your local school system, please help get this alternative way to invest into your children and grandchildren's schools.

Do you want to make a huge difference for your future descendants and their descendants? If so, do this exercise: Write down a list of your descendants, including the youngest, the babies. You have the power to take steps to *stop* their future dependence on Social Security. Do you want to change the world? Start at home with your own loved ones! Now is the time to help your heirs earn money and start their Free Market Roths.

Children can earn an income doing various jobs, such as: household chores, cutting grass, babysitting, etc. Check with your tax preparer as to the annual earnings maximum allowed because the amount and formula changes annually. Seeing they are so young, you do not need to invest the maximum, but they must somehow *earn* the money. However, the money invested doesn't need to be the same money as what was earned—it could be a grandparent's money. If a ten-year-old child earns $1,000 a year by having some type of job—babysitting, cutting grass, a newspaper route or something similar—consider placing $1,000 a year, possibly grandma's money, into the grandchild's Roth each year for 15 years until he is through college. Then, as a young man, he continues to contribute $1,000 a year into his Roth. If this money is invested in a hypothetical growth asset class mutual fund with a historical average annual return of 9% and the investor has a 10% tax rate at age 67, which would you rather have, a Roth, an IRA, or Social Security income? The Roth's total $57,000 after tax contributions would grow *tax-free*, and at his future age of 67, would be worth approximately $1,634,000, which he can withdraw during his lifetime, 100% *tax-free*.

If the ten-year-old had put the same amount of money in a tax-deferred traditional IRA and invested it the same way, he would have $163,000 less at 67 years of age because he would need to pay taxes on 100% of the IRA's appreciation. If Social Security were even available 57 years from now, would you rather have your grandson draw an annual 4-5% off his $1,634,000 or collect Social Security when he retires, if it's even an option? Not a hard decision, is it?

Now is the time to help all your loved ones, including the youngest children and grandchildren, stop depending on the government to take care of their future retirement needs. Be their role model and guardian. Successful stress-free Investors want financially freedom, so no matter what happens, they are capable of financially taking care of themselves. Because of your proper planning and using the Free Market broadly diversified investing philosophy, all your descendants can have sufficient retirement income.

What a fantastic benefit of being financially free! Your children could help their children and grandchildren open and fund their own Roths with their future unneeded Social Security money, or maybe even donate their Social Security checks to their favorite ministries. Investing wisely makes better stewards of God's wealth. Think of all the good that might be accomplished with all the excess that could be given away. Help your children and grandchildren learn that compounding wealth definitely makes more wealth than you can make, or the government can give you. More wealth means more giving! More giving and sharing means more fulfillment, more happiness, more contentment, and more...financial peace of mind!

Do to others as you would have them do to you.

– Luke 6:31

5

Financial Peace of Mind is Your Decision

The heart of the discerning acquires knowledge; the ears of the wise seek it out.

– Proverbs 18:15

Discovering Peace of Mind

We were tired of making other people rich while our assets went nowhere. Jerry and I (Phyllis) just wanted a comfortable lifestyle and to be able to give to our favorite Christian ministries along the way, especially when we graduated to everlasting glory. It didn't seem like that was too much to ask.

Having four teenagers, working full time as an adapted aquatics special education teacher, and going to Eastern Michigan University three nights a week to obtain my Special Education Master's Degree, I already felt pretty well booked. Nevertheless, we agreed that we had to learn more about the right way to invest if we were ever going to be able to afford to retire. I volunteered to do the research. Jerry volunteered to make supper on Thursdays, the one week night I didn't attend graduate school, which freed me up to go to the library and start reading about how investing works.

I loved the challenge! Here was a topic I really was interested in but knew nothing about, so I eagerly started sharing what I was researching with my special education colleagues, teachers and other professional peers at school. They brought me their personal financial questions to research, and after four years of helping other women at school, I lost my teaching job. In 1982, 2,000 teachers in the Detroit area were pink-slipped due to major cutbacks. Many special education teachers were not contracted positions, so each year we were rehired after the federal funding came through, therefore we did not build seniority. I felt that God had dealt me lemons. I was asking the questions, "Why me?" rather than, "What for?" The adapted aquatics program I had developed had been given to a football Coach—someone who never taught swimming or adapted aquatics ever before, and to top that off, he wasn't certified to teach in the Special Education program! I was devastated. Now what would I do?

The staff members I had helped with their investment questions said, "Phyllis, don't look for another special education job, but teach investing to women!" That was an answer from heaven. YES! That was it! It was like God was writing this on my heart! The "What for?" question had been answered. Thanks, ladies! Thank you God!

What a great idea! I loved teaching, and now all I had to do was change my focus to money and investing! So, I looked around, interviewed, and decided on working with a large broker dealer firm that focused on financial planning for the Investor, not on selling products and active trading—or so I thought. I passed all my securities licensing tests, became a financial educator and registered representative, also called an "investment consultant." I was determined to find out the truth about investing.

Boy was I shocked again! The broker dealer only allowed me to put Investors' money into their proprietary "house" mutual funds and proprietary "house" insurance. It was not long before Investors were not happy with their investments or insurance options and asked me to broaden my horizons, so the search began for better and more appropriate investment options.

I began my quest for finding investment *truths* but realized I really needed a different type of company. I shared my frustrations and explained to my Investors that I was looking for the best way for Jerry and I to invest, and they were welcome to come with us on our journey.

Over the next 18 years, our Investors moved eight times. Yes, we moved to eight different broker dealers. I was determined to find the elusive investment *truths*. Each company gave us promises, but once we moved our accounts over, it was the same problems all over again; the Investor was not first, the broker dealer was always first!

Our Investors and I needed a company with ethics that integrated with our Christian beliefs, and to find that in the financial world would be a challenge. I knew that if there were a company out there that did what we needed, God would help us find it. I just kept asking Him to help, as I had no idea where to find this company or philosophy.

So, we kept moving from broker dealer to broker dealer! It became a joke in my office, almost every other year Investors would ask, "When do we sign the papers to move again?" They were just as anxious as we were to find the right investment company, as they wanted what we wanted, financial peace of mind. Our Investors were our best supporters during this very long search.

Finally, we realized the broker dealers were a huge part of the problem. We had to divorce their way of doing business, yes... leave them all behind! None of them could give us the *truths* of investing integrated with our Christian virtues.

For a while, our quest seemed to be futile, as we just couldn't locate any investment company or money manager that could fit our beliefs. We started thinking there might be no company or philosophy out there to match our needs.

Let the peace of Christ rule in your hearts, since as members of one body you were called to peace. And be thankful. Let the word of Christ dwell in you richly as you teach and admonish one another with all wisdom... with gratitude in your hearts to God. And whatever you do, whether in word or deed, do it all in the name of the Lord Jesus, giving thanks to God the Father through him.

— Colossians 3:15-17

It is amazing how you must first have faith by deciding to shut one door in order for another to open. We needed to leave behind the broker dealer community in order to find the answer to our investment search and to gain peace of mind. We needed to teach first ourselves and then our Investors how to stop experiencing information overload, which results in frustration and complexity. We felt we really needed this, especially for our mature women Investors, who typically had shorter work histories, smaller paychecks, and definitely couldn't afford to make investing mistakes or lose money. We wanted to help women just like our families and ourselves, Investors searching for investment *truths* and financial fulfillment.

In 1999, our firm became an independent fee based Michigan Registered Investment Advisor, separating ourselves from all broker dealers, and we started using an active money manager. Becoming independent was wonderful, but using an active money manager was another huge mistake. If you remember 1999, with 20/20 hindsight...the market was good, but very volatile, and our new active money manager bought and sold our investments repeatedly, trying to time the market. The cost of our trading expenses caused us all to lose a lot of money while the market actually did pretty good. We were all very upset! We felt like our accounts were being churned with the frequent buys and sells. We needed the market timing, gambling, and speculating stopped, as we still needed financial peace of mind. Then we heard about the Free Market Portfolio Theory. Could this be what we had been searching 18 years for? We checked it out.

As the chairperson for a national conference in 2000, I invited Mark Matson, a Free Market money manager to speak at the conference. He had a completely different approach, a simplified and easy-to-understand philosophy and process. After hearing his presentation, we realized we had finally found a firm that could help us understand and teach the *truths* of investing to our Investors! We were on our way to fulfilling what we had been searching 18 years for!

What a relief! We finally found a firm we could work with, that understood both the Investor's problems and the Advisor's problems. This philosophy could help us all gain greater peace of mind while getting market returns with less risk and lower costs. Moreover, the global diversification was at least two to four times broader than what we could currently offer our Investors. This is what we needed, an investment process that was simple, better and cheaper!

And we were blessed, the Free Market Portfolio Theory integrated well with the Christian ethics that we and many of our Investors had, and that was extremely important to us. Our prayers were answered! We had found an investment philosophy that was simplified and stress-free, something even I, a kindergarten and special education teacher, could understand. You'll soon understand why! We were elated! Our Investors were contacted and offered the Free Market philosophy. They also were elated!

Be sure you know the condition of your flocks, give careful attention to your herds; for riches do not endure forever, and a crown is not secure for all generations.

— Proverbs 27:23-24

Simpler, Better, and Cheaper

Todd learned about Modern Portfolio Theory (MPT) in his accounting classes in college. Now married and the father of four children, he understood he needed better diversification than he could accomplish on his own investing. He definitely tried. Todd was using retail mutual funds, and doing the best job he could, attempting to diversify his portfolio into multiple asset classes and also used a couple index funds, but he knew he needed help from professionals. Once he learned about the availability of the Free Market philosophy, which utilizes the Modern Portfolio Theory, Todd immediately decided to move his family's portfolio to it. When his investment analysis was completed, Todd could see how poorly his portfolio was diversified, that his market risk was too high, and that his portfolio returns were too low for his family's lifetime goals.

His overlap analysis was very revealing and surprised him. Here is a highly educated businessperson who was unable to structure his own portfolio appropriately according to MPT and the Three Factor Model. Within his retail mutual funds, Todd's analysis had an eight-page, single-spaced list of stocks and bonds that were being duplicated, costing him a lack of prudent global diversification, excess expenses and higher risks. Todd knew there was a better way to invest using the Nobel Prize winning MPT, but he didn't realize it could not be accomplished with retail mutual funds. Fortunately for his family, he was open to change and willing to learn.

> *The sad reality is that most Investors don't even know there is a simpler, better, and cheaper process to being a successful Investor.*

We don't expect you to know how to develop and correlate your own portfolio; however, this chapter will give you a good start on the fundamental basics of the Free Market investment philosophy. Don't think you have to do this all on your own, you don't! Your Coach works with a money manager, an institutional investment company, and a custodian to accomplish this for you. However, we want you to understand the philosophy.

You will quickly see its simplicity and how you don't need to know all the details, just the big picture. It is amazing to realize that once you understand the big picture, the details reveal themselves. It is as easy as making a salad. We hope that our humble illustrations and stories will bring clarity to you.

Have you ever made or eaten a salad? We will use the Seven Layer Salad, as it would have been difficult to have lived through the 1980s without being offered this salad at a church potluck or any gathering of friends. If you understand this salad, or in fact any salad, you will understand the simplified basics of the global markets.

The Seven Layer Salad doesn't just have seven ingredients; it really has at least eleven ingredients. All the individual ingredients (except the mayonnaise) are pure and unique ingredients. The celery is 100% pure celery, not a mixture of 33% peas and 66% celery. The onion is 100% pure onion, not a blend of 50% cheese and 50% onion. Moreover, the salad needs each ingredient in specified amounts. The salad without all the unique eleven plus ingredients in the right proportions wouldn't taste right. Just like you wouldn't want diluted or duplicated ingredients in your salad, you also need to make sure you don't dilute or duplicate stocks and bonds (assets) in your investment portfolio. Duplication reduces the efficiency and returns, of the very most important determinant of your portfolio's returns, prudent diversification.

You need to understand your portfolio's diversification. Just like the Old Testament shepherds needed to know everything about their assets, their flocks (Proverbs 27: 23-24), you need to know about your assets. How different and unique are your investments? Do you know if all the stocks and bonds in your investment portfolio are as pure and unique as the salad ingredients so there is limited duplication? Do you know what you are invested in?

How many different asset class categories are you invested in? Each asset class category of stocks and bonds has its own level of risk. Risk isn't always bad, it just needs to be acknowledged and managed. As we already said, without risk, you can't keep up with inflation, and you could lose purchasing power. No risk equals no growth and no appreciation! Managed risk is good! Your risk tolerance combined with your specific goals' timeline determines how much risk you need.

How does your Advisor manage the risk in your portfolio and keep multiple mutual funds and annuities from duplicating stocks and bonds that you already own in the your other funds and annuities? Or doesn't he? Have you ever asked your Advisor? If you haven't asked or don't know, you need to find out.

You must make a decision. Do you want financial peace of mind? If so, you must know about your assets. Only once you know the truths only then can you control your portfolio risks. Chapter 7 gives you a list of questions to ask your Advisor so you'll be able to get to know your Advisor and your investments better.

Yours, O LORD, is the greatness and the power and the glory and the majesty and the splendor, for everything in the heaven and earth is yours. Yours, O LORD, is the kingdom; you are exalted as head over all. Wealth and honor come from you; you are the ruler of all things. In your hands are strength and power to exalt and give strength to all.

– I Chronicles 29:11-12

As we have already mentioned, and this bears repeating, *everything belongs to God, He created and owns it all...* including the market. You are the trustee of His wealth, and you need to understand how He creates wealth using the market, without anyone intervening. Yes, without stockbrokers, insurance agents, and broker dealers! You will learn how to take advantage of the market to create wealth the way no other strategy does.

If you believe that God made everything good, why is it that the typical Investor's portfolio only has a small portion of the market and not the global market? What about socially responsible investments? Is only part of the market good for Investors and not the rest? Doesn't God use both the good and the bad to benefit His family? Shouldn't we do the same? Who are we to decide what God will cause to prosper or not? There are companies that make weapons and alcohol, does that mean they'll not prosper? If rich people drink alcohol or use guns, won't you take their tithing and charitable gifts for your favorite ministries? God does not have sovereignty only over Biblically responsible markets. He has control of the whole world. You need to be invested in the global market.

This philosophy uses the *global market*, not just a portion of it and believes the market is unpredictable, or random. The market is efficient...that means that no matter if good or bad happens in the world, the market prices will adjust on their own, immediately and automatically. Once you determine that you believe the market is random, your investing strategy will also be determined. Investing in the global market is common sense, because no one knows what sector of the market will do well in the upcoming months and years. It is prudent to be continuously broadly diversified throughout the world, so when the market moves, you are already invested there.

Do you know if your portfolio is diluted with duplicating stocks and bonds? You need to know this so you can take action to eliminate your inadequate diversification and dilution, as it is wasting your precious time and money. The financial media and the big investment companies continually advertise that the way to invest is through asset allocation and diversification. Their message is excellent, but sadly, they don't walk their talk. We found out the hard way, so listen and learn from our mistakes. The mutual funds and variable annuities they publicize and put Investors' money into are duplicating stocks and bonds the Investors already own. Investors are needlessly paying extremely high hidden costs when the same assets are simultaneously bought and sold by many different money managers, some buying while others are selling the identical stock or bond.

The mainstream investment industry does not want you to know this. It'll hurt their business. The more you share this information with other Investors, the more people you can help. Please share this book and help save other Investors from abuse.

Many Investors are trying to make the same changes you are making, but they are afraid of repeating the same investment mistakes they have previously endured. Don't be afraid, have the courage to change! Look forward, not behind. Don't focus on your past negative investment experiences, look anew to the future—a better tomorrow. We all have made investment mistakes, but you didn't know then what you know now—move forward to a brighter tomorrow. Your investment cup is half-full, not half-empty. Think about your growth possibilities! Don't be afraid of change... life is a wonderful journey.

Forget the former things; do not dwell on the past.
See, I am doing a new thing!
– Isaiah 43:18-19

Four-Step Investing Process Overview

The following is a quick and simple "big picture" overview of what you need to know to be a successful stress-free lifetime Investor! Some information might be a review. We believe frequent repetition enhances learning. You personally are not expected to physically implement these steps; however, you do need to understand why the process needs to be followed.

You must first make a decision about your market belief and then your Free Market Coach will make sure the rest of the process is completed. We expand these points a little further in the following chapter for those who require a few more details. Right-brained Investors, please read the next chapter also, as this chapter is just an overview.

#1. Free Markets Work

You must start the process by discovering your beliefs. Once you know your beliefs only then can you step forward and apply them, or act in faith and follow your beliefs.

We believe that markets work. God created everything, including an efficient random market. "Efficient" means that the market does what it does... perfectly, without human forecasting, human second-guessing or human intervention. "Random" means that good things happen (Berlin Wall torn down) and bad things happen (9/11) worldwide, and they all affect the market, which adjusts with new information. No one but God knows what the future holds.

The opposite belief is that markets "fail" and that they can be accurately predicted. Markets "fail" Investors use active money management, which incorporates frequent buying and selling, stock picking, market timing, and track record investing. These strategies lead to frequent moving of your investments, stock tips, and smaller returns due to higher expenses.

The efficient passive philosophy incorporates: *no* market timing, *no* individual stock picking, *no* frequent moving of money, *no* expensive hidden fees, *no* surrender charges, as of this writing...*no* mutual fund scandals, *no* information overload, *no* confusion, delivers global market or better returns, and smaller tax deductible expenses. Yes, we are passionate about sharing this good news with you! For us, pure joy and investment freedom and happiness is Free Market investing!

This philosophy embraces the randomness and unpredictability of the market and helps you avoid frequent investor losses and scandals. Historically, the Free Market portfolio returns are consistently as good as and sometimes even better than the market itself. It seeks to represent the global market, and currently owns over 12,000-plus different stocks and bonds in 40 plus different countries. We'll show you how to get into your globally diversified portfolio and stay there for generations. Yes, buy and hold... forever!

> ### *Time is truly one of the best friends every Investor can have!*

Time is your buddy! Use it to your advantage... *now*! Start investing in the globally diversified Free Market philosophy as soon as you can invest $100 a month. Share your knowledge with others so more Investors can be fulfilled and experience authentic happiness! Be generous with your knowledge and blessings. God rewards generosity.

Command them to do good, to be rich in good deeds, and to be generous and willing to share.
In this way they will lay up treasure for themselves as a firm foundation for the coming age, so that they may take hold of the life that is truly life.
— I Timothy 6:18-19

#2. Diversify with Modern Portfolio Theory

Once you know your belief, the second step is to understand prudent diversification, as that's what gives you better investment returns. The way to get better diversification is to create your portfolio like the Seven Layer Salad. Just as each unique ingredient is necessary in the right amount for the total combined taste, each asset class in the global investment market is necessary for obtaining—at a minimum—market returns. By investing in a broad global diversified portfolio, your portfolio's market risk is managed and reduced.

When you make the Seven Layer Salad, do you want only three to four ingredients, or do you prefer 11 or more different ingredients? Do you want the same amount of onions as you have lettuce? Of course not, you want everything in the correct proportion. The same is true of the asset classes in your portfolio. A *truly prudently* diversified portfolio correlates each of its asset classes, with a targeted amount for each risk level that correlates with your risk tolerance.

Each institutional growth asset class mutual fund has to purchase at least 80% of its funds (or assets) in the one major level of risk or asset class suggested by its name. Just like the onion in the salad is all onion, a domestic large company growth stock mutual fund, for example, will only be allowed to contain only one kind of stock, domestic large company growth stock. Generally, no other types of stocks or bonds are allowed to be held by the fund. Therefore, the name of each the institutional asset class mutual fund matches the asset class it holds.

Here is another example: an international large company growth mutual fund can only hold international companies that are of a capitalization size that fit into the large company asset class size requirements. The majority of international stocks held must be stocks whose earnings are growing, not distressed or value companies. Simplified, an asset class mutual fund invests in exactly what the mutual fund's name says. What a concept. The simple *truth!*

The concept of Free Markets has been around for a long time. Its history goes back to 1776 when Adam Smith wrote *The Wealth of Nations,* stating that markets work, as supply and demand is the best determinant of values, and that prices move randomly. In 1934, Benjamin Graham wrote *Security Analysis,* saying that stock picking worked and that markets fail...however in 1976, before Graham died, he acquiesced some on his Investment Philosophy. In 1965, Paul Samuelson an early proponent of Smith said that price movements are random and unpredictable and that no one can predict what stocks will do. In 1952, Harry Markowitz identified a statistical, scientific way to build diversification into a portfolio called "Modern Portfolio Theory." However, this Nobel Prize winning broadly global diversification strategy needed institutional asset class mutual funds but they were too expensive and only large institutions could afford the $2,000,000 minimum investment into each institutional asset class. Fortunately, for the typical investor, in the early 1990s, the institutional asset class funds became affordable to the average investor through fee Advisors.

To make investing manageable, we recommend using consolidated groups. Funds like these contain various institutional asset class mutual funds; therefore, they are mutual funds holding other mutual funds, or funds of funds. Each fund of funds is highly disciplined and unique: consisting of other asset class domestic and international stock and bond funds.

A domestic stock fund would hold different and unique domestic institutional asset class mutual funds, an international stock fund would hold different and unique international asset class mutual funds, and a bond fund would hold a variety of different and unique fixed income institutional asset class mutual funds. Saving for your future is all about not making common mistakes and not losing value. Having three distinct consolidated funds that cover the broad global market of thousands of stocks and bonds is a stress-free low risk strategy.

*Folly delights a man who lacks judgment, but a man of
understanding keeps a straight course.*

– Proverbs 15:21

#3. Rebalance

The third step is about maintaining your portfolio through rebalancing. All asset classes have market cycles, and rebalancing uses those cycles to follow the number one investing rule to your advantage.

> *The number one rule of successful investing is to buy
> equities at a low price, hold them over a long period,
> and sell them at a high price.*

Your money manager manages and rebalances your portfolio for you, using the funds of funds, which are available only from your Free Market Coach. The money manager correlates dissimilar market cycle asset classes, as asset classes react differently in the market. With the different risk levels moving opposite or dissimilar to each other, your portfolio can get better returns with lower risks. The money manager determines target percentages for each of your account's risk levels, or asset classes based on the Modern Portfolio Theory formula. When one asset category in your portfolio appreciates beyond its stated target, its gains are rebalanced (selling high and the excess moved) to another asset risk level that is below the correlation target, therefore supporting the lower target value (buying low).

Another way the portfolios can be rebalanced is with new money that comes into the funds from new Investors' deposits. This provides even more tax efficiency for all the Investors.

Rebalancing by your money manager puts your portfolio back to its original "target" percentage, thereby maintaining your proportions and resetting your portfolio for more future potential growth. Quoting Professor Malkiel again, "rebalancing a portfolio improves its return by 1 and 1/3 percentage points per year versus a strategy of making no changes."

> *The end of a matter is better than its beginning, and*
> *patience is better than pride.*
> — *Ecclesiastes 7:8*

#4. Stop Moving Your Money... Forever!

Look in the mirror! You are your own worst enemy when you chase returns and move your money! Once you are prudently diversified, stop moving your money... *forever!* Changing your portfolio or chasing hot investment tips is expensive. It can be hard to go against all the media hype. Resist the feeling that you should "do something" when the market changes. Don't listen to and don't believe the hype. Most of all...don't panic! We repeat again... *time is your friend!* Free Market investing is a lifetime strategy. Stay committed to being disciplined and teaching your loved ones to also stay disciplined. You'll be rewarded!

Each time your money moves in and out and between mutual funds, it costs you. It is next to impossible to make up the huge costs of the buys and sells—called turnover—and other hidden costs in investment returns. Your diversification also suffers when you move your money, as your account takes on higher risks, which result in lower returns. You lose again! It is so very important to get prudently diversified and then just stop moving your money! The longer your globally diversified portfolio stays continually and prudently invested and doesn't trade—except to rebalance—the better your returns can be and the lower your investment risk.

Remember how the Seven Layer Salad tastes better when it sits for at least a day? The whole is greater than its parts; it needs to "marinate" the individual tastes together. Time helps the salad, just as time helps your money in the Free Market portfolio. We repeat: *time is truly one of your best investment friends.* Once prudently invested, stay put!

You don't need to know how to rebalance, but you do need to know why it needs to be done. Your money manager manages your portfolio for you. However, you need to take all the classes your Free Market Coach offers. Please teach your heirs so you and they all gain the knowledge needed to maintain the necessary discipline. This will help you have an abundant and stress-free life!

> *My son, do not despise the LORD'S discipline and do not resent his rebuke, because the LORD disciplines those he loves, as a father the son he delights in.*
>
> *— Proverbs 3:11-12*

The Free Market philosophy might be the last investment change you and your descendants will ever need to make. Not just you, but also your children, their children, and your grandchildren's heirs. Get the idea: it's for long-term investing... to the end of time! Only participate in the philosophy if you believe in it. Which investment management style do you believe in?

Peace of mind comes when your behaviors—your actions—match your beliefs.

Once you know you agree with these beliefs and invest accordingly, you can stop worrying about your financial future because you'll understand what you need to know. The rest of the "noise" in the financial world isn't important for your financial peace of mind. Take control of your future by implementing the simple Four-Step Investing Process to becoming a successful investor. You'll make better investment decisions from now on. Never again feel the need to wonder if your money is working hard enough, if you are missing out on the market, or that you need to know everything about the confusing information the media and financial community send out your way.

You just need to know the right information! If you feel you absolutely must read, watch, or listen to the TV and radio gurus, do it only for your entertainment and laugh a lot because you know enough to see through their hype and "noise". They don't have a clue about this better alternative way to invest. It's a lifestyle change.

Now that you know the basics, it is time to look at how this all "marinates." You need to know more reasons why changing to the Free Market Portfolio Theory can give you an enviable stress-free lifestyle.

REVIEW: Four-Step Investing Process

#1. Free Markets Work

#2. Diversify with Modern Portfolio Theory

#3. Rebalance

#4. Stop Moving Your Money...Forever!

Relax... you'll not be tested on this material... so let's dig in and get passionate on why it is best to change your investment philosophy, integrate it with scripture, and tell a few more stories! We'll make the complex simplified, we promise! We'll reduce it to its simplest level.

Whoever gives heed to instruction prospers,
and blessed is he who trusts in the LORD.
— Proverbs 16:20

6

Successful Investors Need to Apply the *Truths*!

Do not conform any longer to the pattern of this world, but be transformed by the renewing of your mind. Then you will be able to test and approve what God's will is—His good, pleasing and perfect will.

— Romans 12:2

You Don't Know What You Don't Know

While talking to a highly intelligent and successful entrepreneurial Investor about why he shouldn't react when the market is down, we realized that Investors who have not completed the Free Market Investor education classes don't know that they don't know! We again encourage you to take every class your Coach offers, as each time you attend, you attain a new level of knowledge and receive what you need to move forward in your understanding. Many of our Investors have attended the same class repeatedly, as each time you are ready for different information. If you don't want to learn and open your mind to new and different ideas, it is difficult to move forward and improve your situation.

For 13 years, I (Phyllis) taught investment classes for a local college and various local community education programs. Many students were highly educated, such as successful business owners, mid to high-level corporate managers, doctors, lawyers, MBAs, nurses, technicians, schoolteachers, retirees and homemakers, all seeking to learn about the successful way to invest. Now we teach at conferences, workshops, churches, businesses and continue to enjoy the student interaction. We ask our students, "Has anyone ever explained to you how to invest simply and stress-free using the Free Market philosophy?" Very few have ever heard of our investing philosophy. Why not? What incentives does the financial world have to teach you investment *truths*? None! It'll only hurt their profit—their bottom line.

Every now and then, an MBA graduate in our classes will say he studied Free Markets and MPT in college but still didn't know how to apply it to his personal investment portfolio. We also have many Advisors attending our classes, as they haven't been taught this strategy by any of their broker dealers. They are also searching for a better way to invest to help their Investors become successful.

How many degrees or how much education you already have doesn't matter. No matter who you are, the media and financial industry don't want you to understand the simplicity of the Free Market. Once you do understand it and act on it, your changed behavior will affect the broker dealers' marketability, as their income stream from your investments will dry up. The buy and hold investment philosophy stops the frequent moving of money, and therefore their income flow stops. Look at the power you have! Once you share this information with other Investors, and they apply the Free Market philosophy, the impact will be that much greater. Knowledge is limiting without the faith actions that support it! It's the actual application of knowledge that is so powerful and can improve the future for generations to come.

As the classes progressed, invariably students would say they never realized how much they didn't know and wondered why Free Market philosophy wasn't taught as part of their high school or college curriculum. We agree! Each generation doesn't need to keep repeating the same common investing mistakes over and over again. Only a few students had been taught anything about investing. Many times, it was only by playing a stock-picking (active trading philosophy) game in high school. Not one student had ever been taught the alternative way to invest—the buy and hold lifestyle investing.

This needs to change during your generation! If you have any middle school or high school education contacts, please share this book with them to help them become aware that there is another way to invest—the non-complex simplified way! The next generation needs to learn about Free Markets, and needs your support. We hope that every conscientious middle school and high school educator reading this book will teach *Stress-Free Investing* to his students! You could change the world and many Free Market Coaches will be happy to help. Please let us know where and when!

> ***...my people are destroyed from lack of knowledge.***
> ***– Hosea 4:6***

Act on Your Beliefs

Knowledge itself will not change your life. Successful Investors don't need to know everything about investing. You just need to know the right things, the *truth*... and then *apply* your knowledge!

Once you complete this chapter and the next, you'll be able to apply the successful process of stress-free lifetime investing. When you commit and move forward, you'll no longer experience the pain of making the same investment mistakes your predecessors made—including us!

That doesn't mean you won't make any mistakes in the future, we are all human, and we all make mistakes, just don't repeat ours. The more mistakes you can avoid the better.

> ## *Application of your new knowledge is a very important step.*

Believing is one thing, but acting on your beliefs is courageous, an act of faith, which is the application and realization of your beliefs. Peace of mind can come from experiencing freedom from investment stress. Yes, *true* abundant lifestyle happiness! Being courageous brings you peace of mind.

Peace is highly emotional and a function of the right brain. Most women are queens of right "braniess" (our word). In the studies of the brain, it has been found that the right brain is the spiritual side of the body, open to oneness with our Creator. Ideally, both sides of the brain work hand in hand with each other, but in each of us one side will dominate. As far as we know, you aren't a brain scientist. If you wish to learn more about right and left brain functions, we encourage you to read the book *My Stroke of Insight*, listed in our Book and DVD List. It is an excellent true story by brain scientist Dr. Jill Bolte Taylor about her own traumatic brain injury and recovery.

Experienced, successful Investors know and have seen their portfolios continue to work through some difficult markets. Their peace comes from the right-brained activities, i.e. seeing the big picture and understanding that as long as you apply the proven strategy, you'll be just fine. Even though peace is not left brained, many left-brained people think they have to analyze and understand exactly what is happening. Therefore, this chapter has a few more process details than the last shorter overview chapter so the left-brained analysts—the detailed people like some of the engineers we work with—are somewhat pacified. We encourage you to seek further explanation in other more technical books such as *Winning the Loser's Game* by Charles D. Ellis and *The Successful Investor Today* by Larry E. Swedroe. These titles are listed on our Book and DVD List.

For the right-brained readers, just read through this chapter. Don't delve in too deep; just get the gist of the material. There is no test! We have found that many of our right-brained Investors need to read this material over a couple times before clearly understanding and becoming comfortable with the complete philosophical change from how they had been previously investing. Don't hesitate, just jump in with both feet and reread this chapter as many times as needed! Please stay curious and courageous. It is good to be inquisitive and to ask questions to obtain clarity. Write down your questions to ask your Free Market Coach.

Women (typically more right-brained) stop to ask driving directions so much earlier than men (typically more left-brained) at least faster than my previously analytic husband Jerry used to! Now that he's retired, Jerry has become more relationship oriented and is doing much better in asking for help earlier. Men, we give you permission to ask questions also!

The downside for many analytics is the feeling that they need to know everything before making a financial decision. Some don't want anyone to know that they don't know, and they won't ask for help, so they freeze up and do nothing, eventually hurting themselves and their families. They are absolutely frozen, paralyzed—no action takes place regarding changing their investment philosophy until they have a master's degree in "Mutual Funds," a master's degree in "Stocks," a master's degree in "Bonds," plus a master's degree in "Annuities." That attitude promotes information overload. Information overload is banned from this point on! It's not needed, not wanted, nor desired. Remember, you seek different results, so you too must change.

He who belongs to God hears what God says.

– John 8:47

You Don't Need to Know Everything

The Free Market philosophy is a simplified concept and easily understood once you let go of your old financial misinformation. Be happy you don't need to know everything! In this chapter, we'll also share some additional things you can stop doing once you change your investment philosophy, as you'll no longer feel you are on active money management information overload. You'll no longer feel that someone knows something you should know. You'll be satisfied that you know what you *need* to know.

In 1977, I (Phyllis) opened my teacher's retirement plan with one of my school district's approved mutual fund representatives. I felt I needed to know everything about investing before I could make a good decision about whether to sign up or not. I called my mutual fund representative every day with a new question. After a week of bothering him, he told me to go and research it myself, as he didn't have time for all my questions. That was some of the best advice I have ever received!

As mentioned before, Jerry suggested I start my research at our local library, so off I went. Reality set in really fast! After reading some technical financial periodicals, and being a right brained non-technical person, I realized there was no way I could comprehend it all before the end of the open enrollment period. I just needed the right information. That was the problem, where was I to get the *truths* of investing?

Even after I studied mutual funds since 1977, and eventually in 1982 entered the financial industry, it still took an additional 18 years to locate our investment philosophy and understand how it integrates with our virtues and scripture. I searched for a book to learn this right-brained material, but I couldn't find one. We finally realized God was telling us that we needed to share the story of His Free Markets and that everyone could easily become a successful investor when integrating their virtues into their investment beliefs, their Investment Philosophy. Therefore, we felt compelled to write this book so you would have the benefit of many Investors' "school of hard knocks!"

What's your history of investing? Everyone comes to investing with some history, even no experience is a history. Jerry and my (Phyllis') history was absolutely "no investing;" we knew how to work, tithe, save, and pay bills, but knew nothing about investing, and we searched for investing knowledge in all the wrong places.

You might be doing the same thing, e.g. asking loyal friends, peers, a spouse, or relatives how they invest and how they think you should invest. There are also many books written about different ways to invest. However, most books don't support the Free Market philosophy. Instead, they support the authors of the books. Please be careful of what you read, hear, believe and apply.

Many Investors are worried about investment scandals, and concerned about their future. They want and need security but are speculating and gambling by allowing their loyal Advisors to market time and pick stocks, bonds and mutual funds based on past historical returns. If you are already on information overload, in this new stress-free process you'll want to "dump" all the old information so you have room for new knowledge.

We hope as you share this book and it gets out to the masses, more and more Investors will apply their new investment knowledge and decide to move to more passive investing and away from active money management. Please make a decision at the end of this chapter. We encourage you to decide to stop allowing and supporting financial abuse. Doing *nothing* is a decision—a decision to keep your status quo and not improve your situation or solve your investing problems. However, moving forward can change your life! You'll have to say "good-bye to some old beliefs. You decide. Please read this chapter with an open mind and willingness to learn. You'll never be the same if you believe and apply your new beliefs.

If you have never heard of Free Markets before reading this

book, that's OK, everyone has to start someplace. It is time to become empowered and enlightened. This strategy is right for every level of Investor, from the beginner, starting out with a $100 a month investment to the experienced multimillionaire.

We wish we had this information many years ago. We wouldn't have made so many investment mistakes and lost so much valuable time. We pray you also agree that it is time for you to learn the alternative way of successful investing and are willing to share it with your family so all their lives can be improved.

Once you better understand this simplified Four-Step process and apply all the steps to your portfolio, you too will gain your own financial peace of mind. Then you'll be able to "forget" the past unnecessary knowledge you have inadvertently accumulated and no longer need.

Did you visualize your goals in Chapter 2 and retirement in Chapter 4? It works and really helps your subconscious mind accept and retain new material, so let's do another quick visualization.

Please visualize putting all your previous (active trading) investment knowledge and experiences into an old beat-up suitcase—one that you'll never need again. Yes, unload it all out of your brain and stuff it in the suitcase! You can expand your suitcase if necessary; just get rid of your information overload. Then put the suitcase out of sight, stashing it in your attic, basement, barn, garage... anywhere out of the way. Seeing this is a "visualization," you can even take that old suitcase and toss it over an ocean, or dig a hole to the center of the earth and put it there! Anything is possible in your visualization. We hope that you will never want to locate and reopen the suitcase again, as then you don't have to remember where you stashed or tossed it.

Putting your old confusing knowledge away will allow your mind to use this available freed up space for new information. Later you'll decide whether to go back to the old suitcase and reclaim all your old information or leave it where you stashed it.

We hope you will move forward, acting on the new information you are learning.

It is time to stop losing your hard-earned money and start investing for your success. We hope you are reading this book to make a positive change in your financial lifestyle, so prepare for it and know that it is possible. When you realize the benefits of the passive strategy and apply the *truths* of investing, your money goes into a globally diversified Free Market buy and hold strategy, which is the opposite from the active trading philosophy.

Books are to be used and enjoyed. Please highlight and add scriptures as you read so you can easily return to your favorite sections. Enjoy! You are taking a fantastic peace of mind trip in this chapter. And yes, we will repeat some.

Blessed is the man who does not walk in the counsel of the wicked or stand in the way of sinners or sit in the seat of mockers. But his delight is in the law of the LORD, and on his law he meditates day and night.

He is like a tree planted by streams of water, which yields its fruit in season and whose leaf does not wither. Whatever he does prospers.

– Psalm 1:1-3

Step #1: Free Markets Work

The Free Markets work perfectly. God made it this way. It has its own timing and is random, so allow it to work for you. No one can predict the US and foreign markets accurately! It is also efficient, as it needs no humans or other entities, especially Wall Street and governmental interference. In fact, it does well in *spite* of human interference. All knowable and predictable information is already in the market price and only unknowable and unpredictable information will move the price going forward. All you need to do is harness the forces of the Free

Markets to create the wealth and the peace of mind you and your loved ones deserve.

Our Investors don't need the media to tell them how to invest, as the media promotes active trading. You know who these companies are; they advertise and pay the media's paychecks. Unless your head has been stuck in the sand for the last 15 years, you already know that the media is *not* your friend. The financial media and Advisors of every size broker dealer prey on and benefit from ill-informed Investors' vulnerability, confusion, and lack of having a lifetime game plan. Their agenda is to make money, lots of money for themselves, not for you, but off you and from you.

Helen Davis Chaitman, attorney for several Madoff victims and a victim herself, when interviewed by Larry Doyle, March 2, 2010 said, "Wall Street will manipulate the laws to enrich itself at the expense of every honest hard-working American taxpayer." We have witnessed and taught this for years. You must become astute, and reading this chapter is the first step to taking back your financial control and eliminating scandals in your life and your family's lives. You need the investment *truths*.

> ### *The LORD detests lying lips,*
> ### *but he delights in men who are truthful.*
> #### *– Proverbs 12:22*

The efficiency of consistently owning global Free Markets allows you to receive market returns and avoid much of the risk and unpredictable characteristics of the markets. We diversify globally by owning investments in 40 plus countries because we don't have the magic formula to predict the market. No one does!

The abusive strategies we'll lightly and quickly review include stock picking, track record investing, market timing, and high turnover. People who believe in these investment strategies believe markets fail and are predictable and inefficient, exactly the opposite to the markets work belief. Investors do not need these abusive techniques to become successful Investors. We'll teach you to stop living in a fantasy world where risk does not happen. Everything has risks, but they can be managed with long-term strategies. Long-term investors tend to pay less attention to short-term performance. The only way to get long-term returns is to be prudently diversified, stay in the market and do not panic.

Keep an open mind so you are able to understand and "see through" inappropriate investment strategies in order to protect yourself. Once you read this chapter, you'll easily see that you do not need these schemes and you can avoid them. Once you are aware then you can easily make good investing decisions.

Scripture speaks openly and frequently about the *truths* of wealth and economics—the good and the bad of money. As you already know, God created and owns it all; therefore, it is important to follow His Word and avoid misfortune.

I have seen a grievous evil under the sun:
wealth hoarded to the harm of its owner, or wealth lost
through some misfortune, so that when he has a son there
is nothing left for him.
– Ecclesiastes 5:13-14

Stock Picking

Sally, one of our new Investors, brought us her divorce settlement, which consisted of half of her ex-spouse's investment accounts. She was very confident that we wouldn't need to change any of her investments, as her ex-spouse was an intelligent and highly educated person. Yes, in his specialty. Sally believed that her ex and his Advisor had set up a well-diversified portfolio of individual stocks and growth mutual funds. However, her unique investment analysis showed that she only had 476 different (unique) stock positions, compared to a possible 12,000+ unique global positions in our portfolios. This was one of the worst inappropriately diversified portfolio we had ever seen! This unbelievable scenario is sadly repeated for many divorcees and widows in the USA. Women; do not abdicate your responsibilities. Stand up for yourselves; you need a globally diversified portfolio! Not being prudently diversified is very risky. Is it worth taking those unnecessary risks? Consider how much money you could lose. How long would it take to recoup those losses? Is it worth the risk? *No!*

Stock picking is a strategy that invests in individual stocks. Either you or your Advisor, usually under the advice of a highly paid investment company's financial analyst, pick the stock. No one, including you or any Advisor or analyst, no matter how many millions they earn a year, knows the future. It doesn't matter if they have a file six inches thick on what every company's stock has done in the past, they don't have a clue what will happen in the future. That's right, not one clue! Don't fall for their persuasive talk! It is impossible for anyone to consistently predict market movements, as markets are random and based on supply and demand. If anyone knew what the best stocks were, do you think they would tell you? They would use it for their own profit, not for yours!

Only God knows the future. Stock picking is gambling and speculating. If you really want to gamble and speculate, go to a casino. The odds are better there than in the market. At least at the casino you can have some excitement while you watch your money leave your control. In stock picking, the money leaves without even a little enjoyment of this fast supposedly wealth building process.

Focusing on building wealth fast does not please God (Proverbs 28:20-22, Proverbs 24:4). Christians prosper and gain happiness when they please and emulate God (Psalm 1:1-3, Proverbs 21:5).

If anyone speaks, he should do it as one speaking the very words of God. If anyone serves, he should do it with the strength God provides, so that in all things God may be praised through Jesus Christ. To him be the glory and the power forever and ever. Amen.

– I Peter 4:11-12

A portfolio of individual stocks makes you more vulnerable than a stock mutual fund, as you can only diversify into as many levels of asset class risks as you have stock. In addition, the risks you accept with picking stocks are unique to that stock, such as embezzlement, change of management, improper acquisitions, inferior products, and inadequate accountability. Do you remember Lehman Brothers, Enron, Tech Stocks and WorldCom? They all had their own unique risks and are prime examples of stock picking being gambling and speculating.

Sam, a stockbroker, was on vacation with his family the same time that Judy, a Coach was also on vacation with her family. The market took a sudden steep slide downwards. This was a crisis in Sam's mind as he constantly watched the market movements on his Blackberry and on TV. For three days, Sam was on his cell phone, selling and buying different stock, trying to protect his Investors by moving them to different sectors of the market. Stock picking is the worst of all possible worlds when making sector bets on what is hot or think *will* be hot. Sam's family didn't see much of him on that vacation. Meanwhile, Judy, a Free Market Coach, was also aware of the market news and kept in contact with her office. Not one concerned Investor called about the market slide. Judy sold nothing and bought nothing as her Free Market Investors already had a disciplined and diversified portfolio for any market. She and her family had a wonderful time together on their vacation. *We repeat, if you feel you must change your portfolio due to market changes, you are probably invested in the wrong portfolio.*

Do you want to reduce stress whenever the market moves?

You can! If you are in an appropriate portfolio, one that is suitable for your risk tolerance and investment objectives, just do nothing when the market moves down. Investors in broadly diversified global portfolios don't feel they need to panic when the market has problems. Free Market investors accept short-term market declines and believe the best course of action is to hold on, staying disciplined during extended bear markets. Hold on forever. Eighty years of market crash historical data tells us the market will recover. It always has. However, you know that past performance is not a guarantee of future results!

Do not listen to forecasters or predictions. If you hear a market forecast, why wouldn't that person already have acted on his forecast? Think about it! Why would they share their knowledge with you before they took advantage of it? Especially if it's a written forecast. By the time you and I hear about it, it is old information and has already affected the market price. How good is a late forecast? Don't fall for gurus who make market predictions and forecasts. You might have heard the analogy that a monkey throwing darts at the Wall Street Journal stock page would outperform the stock traders whose job it was to pick future performing stocks. It might be true!

Stock picking eliminates prudent global diversification! If you believe you are picking the best individual stocks, then you are leaving out other stocks that are essential for prudent global diversification. Just don't pick individual stocks. Get prudently globally diversified and hold that course.

It doesn't matter how smart you are, how many initials you have behind your name, or how many degrees you have, you always will have less diversification with individual stocks unless you buy 12,000-plus domestic and global stocks and bonds in over 20-plus different unique asset classes! But here is another problem, how much do you buy of each? The good news is...you don't need to do this by yourself. You just need to understand how important diversification and correlation are. We'll discuss these more later.

Whoever trusts in his riches will fall, but the righteous will thrive like a green leaf.

– Proverbs 11:28

Track Record Investing

I admit it, I (Phyllis) have done track record investing in the past! When I was working through a broker dealer, we used many different but well-known mutual fund families: Fidelity, Idex, Putnam, MFS, Fidelity Advisors, Franklin-Templeton, amongst others, as some of the growth funds had decent historical track records. During our Investor meetings, we would review how the Investor's portfolio did over the previous one to ten years, and determine to keep it in the portfolio or replace it. The investment's track record was key to making the decision. Fortunately, in 2000 we found that the Free Markets work and have been helping our Investors stay disciplined in prudently diversified portfolios ever since.

Track record investing is another abusive strategy that active money managers use. It is the process of looking at how an investment has done historically over time, and then deciding to invest in it because of its previous historical track record. The *truth* is, the magic never lasts! You cannot buy past performance, and history has proven that performances after the good years are typically very poor. Predicting future returns by counting on historical returns is like driving your car forward while looking in your rear-view mirror. Don't do it!

Track record investing does not work. No stocks, bonds, mutual funds nor asset class will consistently repeat its previous returns. History used another way can give us a bigger picture. Have you ever thought of asking the financial media to look at historical returns and tell you how their previous predictions turned out or how well their "hot" top funds did over the years?

Using Morningstar historical data, we can do a unscientific "hypothetical" study of best ten mutual funds' returns from 1992 to 2000. We want look at how well the top ten funds performed over eight years, using $100,000 as a starting value and the top ten funds' actual historical 1992 annual returns. Starting in January 1993, the top ten mutual funds of 1992 were hypothetically purchased by putting $10,000 into each of the top ten 1992 funds, and then, if they did not maintain any position on the top ten mutual fund list for that same year, sold off December 31, 1993.

Every year this process repeated. January 1, the previous year's top 10 mutual funds were purchased with the December 31 liquidated values of the previous year's top ten account values and reinvesting those amounts into the new top 10 mutual funds of the year just completed. This process was repeated annually for eight years, to December 31, 2000.

The $100,000 grew to $192,330.53. However, not one of the top ten mutual funds qualified to remain on the top ten funds list two years in a row. Therefore, every mutual fund was sold off each December 31, incurring commissions, expenses and realizing taxes or losses.

After $86,830.10, eight years of taxes, were deducted, the top ten fund's "hypothetical" Investors received a disappointing 3.53% after tax and after expense return! Even worse was the portfolio's risk! The risk, also called standard deviation or volatility, of this portfolio was 44.41%! The higher the number, the higher the risk. The S&P 500's risk is approximately 20.6%, therefore the top ten fund portfolio was more than 2 times riskier than the S&P 500 and gave the Investors only a 3.53% return! This hypothetical portfolio of investing in last year's best investments had too much risk with too little a return!

Don't look to the past to predict the future! Obtaining wealth takes time, patience, and continuous prudent diversification.

A stingy man is eager to get rich and is unaware that poverty awaits him.

– Proverbs 28:22

Market Timing

We also tried market timing... once, back in the mid-1990s. Our broker dealer had a relationship with an independent market timer, supposedly a person with a great track record of success. The market timer talked a good story. We offered his services to some of our larger Investors to see if they could get better returns. We had a few willing Investors agree to try his services, during our search to find the "answer," the *true* way to invest. It was a short-lived experiment. None of the market timing Investors received better returns than those without the market timer's expertise, so within three years, we fired the market timer. Our Investors were so very happy to get rid of the market timer and his additional fees.

Market timing is choosing to get in and out of the market, or allowing someone else to decide when to move your money between the different asset classes or sectors, at their will. Getting out of the market is easy, but knowing when to get back in is the hard part. Not getting back into the market is devastating to your bottom line as your portfolio cannot grow without being in the market. Market timing is another abusive investment strategy that has no evidence of working for the benefit of the Investor. The market timer wins, and you, the Investor, lose!

Much of the information you receive from the media is market timing, which destroys prudent diversification. Be wary of advice on the Internet and TV channels, as it is typically partial and inaccurate information. Moving your money is extremely harmful to your financial wealth.

> *Moving in and out of the market in response to market volatility insures you are selling at the wrong time, and you will pay the price for this inappropriate activity.*

When someone tells you they do technical or tactical asset allocation, that means they do market timing just by using different quantitative measures. Avoid them! No one can successfully market time, no one.

Ten-year studies by the Fact Set Research Systems (2003) have shown that just being out of the Market for ten of the best market days (days the market goes up) during the ten years will reduce your returns approximately by half. Being out of the market 20 of the best market days during the ten years will give you a return of .24%, and being out of the market during 30 of the best market days will result in a return of -3.07%. That means if you started with $10,000 ten years ago, and you stayed out of the market those 30 best market days, your $10,000 would be down to $7,348, a huge loss for not being in the market!

But worse, some Investors have missed the whole market uptick—by being out of the market over 60 days of the best market—which caused their $10,000 to be reduced to $3,359 because they moved out of the market and stayed out too long. When do you know there was a good day? After it happens—the next day!

Market timing involves being right twice, once when you decide to get out, and then again when to get back into the market. Your normal human emotions tend to lead you in the wrong direction. When the market is high, you are typically optimistic. However, when the market is low, you are pessimistic. The odds of being able to time the market successfully are not good. It's actually speculating. The best place to speculate is in the casinos with discretionary money, not in the market with your future.

To quote Dr. Charles Ellis' book again, he stated, "The evidence on investment managers' success with market timing is impressive – and overwhelmingly negative." Please don't gamble with money you need in the future.

The best thing you can do to be a successful Investor is

change your behavior. Being in the market is one of the most important ingredients of investing. Invest in the broadly diversified Free Market and stay there, forever, as the market does much better without any interference. Once your portfolio is truly prudently and broadly diversified, stay put. Be patient! You'll be rewarded.

A faithful man will be richly blessed, but one eager to get rich will not go unpunished.

– Proverbs 28:20

Investment Costs

I (Maria) am the type of person who feels secure when I'm in control and well informed. When working as a biomedical photographer, I'd read my employers' 401(k) approved investment prospectuses, and then believe I could make an informed decision. I frequently logged into my 401(k) account to check my investments and then decided to make changes to my allocation or portfolio, because of the returns. I never realized how I was hurting myself. I was poorly diversified, creating more investment costs, lowering my account's returns, buying high and selling low, as I was ineffectively chasing returns. I had no idea that I was actually killing my returns while trying to improve them. In reality, I was going backward and being my own worst enemy. Nobody was doing this to me; I was doing it all to myself, creating more stress with my counterproductive behavior. Now, investing within our disciplined philosophy is a much different experience. I am using the academic research that supports buying and holding a globally diversified, passively managed Free Market portfolio. This strategy achieves market returns with lower risk and as a result this also lowers my stress and my investment expenses.

Portfolio underperformance is frequently the result of excessive costs. Investors in actively traded funds have no knowledge of their actual investment costs because most of the costs are hidden. Costs matter and have a devastating effect on the performance of your portfolio. Sadly, most Investors do not know how to control their costs or their risks. You can control costs, just as you can control risks, but most Investors look at returns instead of the other investment aspects.

Some of your investment costs might even go towards your Advisor's rewards. Does your Advisor win nice trips, corporate or broker dealer funded vacations? If you don't know, ask him who pays for his trips. Does your investment company advertise? Ask your Advisor who pays for their advertisements. Again, *follow the money!* If he says the broker dealer pays for his trips and the ads, you know the real *truth*: you helped pay for the Advisors trips and the advertisements.

Why don't you know this? The active money management companies and their Advisors don't want you to know. Investment companies need you to move between mutual funds and keep moving, as that creates income for them. This is also true for individual stocks. Why do you think these ads on the TV promote daily stock trading for a low cost? This is another WIN-LOSE. They win by getting richer, while you lose by paying more and more hidden costs, thereby getting poorer and poorer. It doesn't matter if you do well or not, they just want you to keep moving your money!

Studies conducted on the average Investor by Dalbar, a highly regarded financial services research firm, show the reason average Investors get inferior portfolio returns is due to imprudent behaviors. Investors get emotional and feel they must react to the market. They feel they must do something! Therefore, to pacify their feelings, they end up moving their money, just like I (Maria) did before I understood how much I was hurting my returns. Over the long haul, just staying invested in the market will give an Investor a possible 8-9% annual market return. However, as we mentioned earlier, according to the "Quantitive Analysis of Investor Behavior, 2010" Dalbar, Inc.

www.dalbar.com, the average equity Investor instead received a paltry 3.17% annual return, and this was before 2.80% inflation and taxes. During the same 20 years, the S & P buy and hold Investors were enjoying a 8.20% annual return before inflation and taxes! Which investor would you rather be? Investors' own behaviors are destroying their long-term returns.

As soon as you broadly diversify and stop moving your money, you could start enjoying the advantages of lower costs. When there are fewer costs taken from your portfolio's value, you'll potentially receive higher returns. The longer you hold your broadly diversified portfolio, the better the chances of obtaining that portfolios historical expected return.

Holding your portfolio for 20 years allows your risk of not obtaining your expected return to lower from its potentially highest risk, years 1 to 6 to its lowest risk, years 15 to 20! Each time you change the risk level composition of your portfolio; your risk vortex starts over at the beginning, at year 1 again, and creates additional costs along with the unnecessary risk. It is impossible to stop mutual fund's active money managers from changing your holdings without your approval. When they change the holdings within your funds, they create larger costs for you. However, you can invest in a different type of mutual fund, the institutional asset class mutual funds, that support the Free Market philosophy.

Mutual funds have many layers of expenses. Expense ratios are only one of these costs. What are your total real annual investment costs? Has your Advisor told you?

Here are the 2009 average annual expense ratios for various types of mutual funds, taken from the 12/31/2009 Morningstar Principia software and the 12/31/2009 DFA software.

Average Annual Expense Ratios:

Domestic Stock Funds:
US Small Value: 1.51%

US Small Blend: 1.42%

Domestic Equity: 1.35%

US Large Value: 1.27%

US Large Blend: 1.24%

International Stock Funds:
Emerging Markets: 1.70%

International Small/Mid Growth: 1.57%

International Equity: 1.55%

International Large Blend: 1.48%

International Small/Mid Value: 1.44%

International Large Value: 1.41%

Bond Funds:
High Yield Bond: 1.21%

World Bond: 1.14%

Intermediate Term Gov't Bond: 1.02%

Ultra Short Bond: .74%

We already told you there is no free lunch...all investments have costs, including the Free Market philosophy. Also, add to your expense ratios any commissions: front, back, or C-share loads; advisory fees; transaction costs; and any mortality risk insurance costs if you own an annuity; plus any unseen intrinsic (hidden costs) for your first year; and then add any recurring portfolio costs for the following years. If your total cost is more than 2%, you are paying excessive costs.

Would you rather have lower tax-deductible investment costs or higher hidden investment costs? Would you build a house without knowing the costs? Listen to Luke, who says you need to know your current costs!

Suppose one of you wants to build a tower.
Will he not first sit down and estimate the cost to see
if he has enough money to complete it?

– Luke 14:28

Turnover Rate

Otto and Grace are missionaries in a foreign country and have a retirement plan through their church—a large worldwide organization with many missionaries and staff. An investment analysis on the church's annuity retirement plan revealed it as one of the worst active trading investments we have ever analyzed! It had high turnover, high risks, high costs, and gave the missionaries high stress! One of the annual turnover rates of at least one of the mutual funds within the annuity was a disastrous annual 1,178%. That means their money manager bought and sold all of their mutual fund's holdings more than 11 times in one year and 78% were bought and sold 12 times! Their investment's costs could be very high, into the double digits! These costs are paid to the investment company before the Investor received any appreciation. This is criminal, and the financial department of this organization should be held accountable. How can a large Christian organization offer such a terrible investment to their unsuspecting employees? This ignorant church administration should be ashamed of itself! They are misusing their responsible position within the organization. They probably don't mean to hurt their employees, but this problem is due to nothing more than a lack of knowledge! If they are ignorant and didn't know the *truths* about what they are offering their employees, they must seek clarity and knowledge and change their behaviors.

Other Christian organizations, including colleges and

churches, have similar inappropriate active trading investment options in their retirement plans. The nonprofit and corporate world needs help understanding that there is an alternative stress-free way to invest and how it integrates with scripture. Many religious organizations are doing a huge disservice to their own servants of God by offering them inappropriate underperforming investment options.

Turnover is the frequency of the buying and selling rate within mutual funds and individual stocks. You must know your mutual funds' turnover rates. Every time there is a transaction, whether you approve it or not, costs are incurred—yes, you pay for those costs, whether you have approved the sales and purchases or not! *Active money managers who buy and sell frequently within mutual funds create higher costs for Investors than money managers who buy and hold.* Mutual fund money managers need to be held accountable for these abusive costs committed at the Investors' expense. It is all about their making money by moving your money. Every time money moves, whether the Investor sells at a gain or loss, the brokerage house wins! Again, *follow the money!*

Always ask your Advisor about the turnover rate of your mutual funds. Each time your mutual fund's money manager buys or sells, your mutual fund expenses increase. Do you understand? That is called *turnover and the Investor pays for it!* Excessive trading and costs are difficult to justify, as they rob you of your returns. Please refer back to Dr. Charles Ellis' quote in chapter 3 where he states that it is very difficult to recoup active trading costs. High turnover costs are detrimental to your returns, as they are paid out first, before you receive your net returns. If you would like to check on the turnover rates for your investments, you can easily do so by checking: www.Morningstar.com or www.Finance.Yahoo.com.

Most investors have no idea what their mutual fund's turnover rates are. Stock funds with annual turnover rates greater than 20% that are not giving the investor any greater return than lower turnover funds should be avoided. Fixed income turnover is greater due to their shorter holds, so keep their turnover ratio under 60% per year. Why invest in costly investments when you can choose designed institutional class funds? If you do not have a computer, you can check every growth mutual fund prospectus you plan to invest in, as the turnover rate is quoted there also.

Here is a comparison from the 12/31/2009 Morningstar Principia and DFA software's, listing the 2009 average annual turnover rates for various types of mutual funds:

Average Annual Turnovers:

Domestic Stock Funds:
Domestic Equity: 94%
US Small Blend: 93%
US Small Value: 83%
US Large Blend: 80%
US Large Value: 70%

International Stock Funds:
International Large Blend: 99%
International Small/Mid Growth: 99%
International Equity: 90%
Emerging Markets: 85%
International Small/Mid Value: 63%
International Large Value: 56%

Bond Funds:
Intermediate Term Gov't Bond: 337%
World Bond: 173%
Ultra Short Bond: 129%
High Yield Bond: 87%

From our experience of doing investment analyses on many mutual funds and annuities, some of the most expensive mutual fund and annuity total annual investment costs could be 6% or higher of the account value, mostly due to their higher turnover. As we stated before, you must know your turnover rate, plus other hidden costs. You need to know if you are paying too much due to high turnovers as then can you make an informed decision. Your portfolio's hidden costs are hard to quantify:

- Bid/ask spread (price difference between the buy and sell prices and what the market maker gets paid)
- Market impact (pressure on price while broker has the trade and then makes the trade)
- Delays (time wasted while the broker waits to execute the trade)
- Missed trades (the broker fails to execute the trade during an upward price movement)

What are your hidden costs?

Lower turnovers rates keep your costs lower which may result in better market returns. You lose peace of mind when you move your money because each time your money moves more than a minimum, your portfolio begins a new time horizon. If you change your investments and/or mutual funds every three years, like the typical Investor, you never get beyond the third year of a 20-year downward risk vortex. Again, you lose and they win! You need a better investment strategy a WIN-WIN-WIN, where everyone wins!

By wisdom a house is built, and through understanding it is established; through knowledge its rooms are filled with rare and beautiful treasures. A wise man has great power, and a man of knowledge increases strength; for waging war you need guidance, and for victory many advisors.

— Proverbs 24:3-6

Step #2: Diversify with Modern Portfolio Theory

Kay wanted to save for retirement and tithe to her favorite ministries. Her investment analysis showed that her retirement plan allowed only five levels of risk for her to invest in—yes, only five different levels of risk also called asset classes: Domestic (US) Large, Domestic Small, International Large, Domestic Bonds, and Money Market. In the first asset class, she had 43 different mutual funds to pick from, money managers all buying the same level of risk, the S&P domestic large companies like IBM, Coke, Cisco, etc. Kay invested in six domestic large company mutual funds, as she correctly determined that she needed growth and liked investing in companies she recognized. However, all the mutual funds she selected were all in the same asset class risk level. Therefore, she was buying the same stocks six times, causing her unnecessary expenses. Besides duplicating much of her portfolio, Kay also was lacking prudent global diversification by not going into the international asset class risk level.

Many Investors are committing the same common investment mistake. Investing in two or more mutual funds that purchase the same stocks or bonds is a wasteful expense. Avoid duplicating your asset categories! In changing her Investment Philosophy to Free Markets, Kay would double or possibly triple her global diversification and her passive money manager would automatically rebalance her account quarterly, as needed. She would therefore also keep true to her correlation targets while saving on her costs, allowing her to feel she could give more to her favorite ministries.

An efficient portfolio incorporates the diversification of Modern Portfolio Theory (MPT), whose developers won the Nobel Prize in economics. MPT is an academic strategy. Harry Markowitz, one of the three Nobel Prize winners, based his "Efficient Frontier" concept on the relativity of risks and returns. His "Efficient Frontier" charts the amount of risk and the returns of each of the various unique asset classes, and then by correlating the dissimilar categories of risk, the portfolio risk diminishes and the portfolio's return increases. These are the basics of MPT, which every ERISA retirement plan should emulate, according to Section 3, pages 10-12 of the Uniform Prudent Investor Act, drafted by the National Conference of Commissioners on Uniform State Laws and approved and recommended for enactment in all the states as of July 29, 1994.

To keep this complex topic simplified, just remember that you ideally need to own the global market, in 20-plus risk levels, always, every day, in up and down markets. Be thankful, a passive money manager can manage this for you. MPT does not eliminate risk, but it does help manage it and allows you to avoid gambling and speculating with volatile segments of the market. You'll not eliminate losses, while on the other hand you'll also not be affected as negatively as the less diversified actively managed Investors. There might even be years where your returns might be lower than the actively traded funds, and that is because this strategy uses global markets and is not heavily concentrated in just a few asset classes. An investment analysis shows that most actively managed Investors invest in only three to four unique levels of risk and 70% to 80% of their portfolio is typically in the US Large Company Growth level of risk. People are comfortable with the familiar big company names like Pepsi, Coke, IBM, Cisco, etc. Do you think this what their money manager's highly paid analyst is also comfortable investing in?

Lack of diversification is unacceptable to a successful Investor as asset allocation explains where the majority of returns come from. You can see the results of poor diversification by looking at what happened to Investors in the past. Investors who lost big in the 2000-2002 market crash lost trillions because their portfolios were invested in too many similar assets. Therefore, the majority of their money responded in tandem, as similar investment categories all went down together in the market cycle. Ask your Advisor to do an investment analysis to see if you are prudently diversified for your risk tolerance. How many asset classes and different levels of risk does your portfolio hold? Do you have similar asset classes or dissimilar asset classes? Do you even know?

MPT is an important component of the Free Market philosophy because no one can predict returns, so you need this strategy of using many different unique institutional asset class mutual funds. Mutual funds are a grouping of stocks and bonds, each with an investment objective and managed by an investment company money manager.

Think of asset classes as ownership of groups of different size and types of domestic and international businesses and bonds: domestic large-growth companies, domestic small-growth companies, domestic large companies with distressed value, domestic small companies with distressed value, domestic very small companies, international large-growth companies, international small-growth companies, international small distressed companies, etc. *Many asset classes are dissimilar to each other, each moving independently from each other, all in different market cycles.* Some asset classes go up in value at the same time as other asset classes go down in value. Just like waves, when their down cycles bottom out, they turn upward, and when their up cycle peeks, they turn downward.

Professor Malkiel states, "There are huge differences in regional returns. Even though the portfolios in the US market actually lost money in the first decade of the 21st century, emerging-market stocks enjoyed returns of more than 10% per year. Every portfolio should have substantial holdings in the fast-growing emerging economies of the world."

Which levels of risk are best? Which ones should you be invested in? Do this quick little exercise.

Asset Class Exercise

Here are eight of the 20-plus different levels of risk, asset classes. Each had an excellent annual return in a certain year. Guess which asset class got the best returns in each year. Draw a line from the year to the name of the asset class. The answers are at the end of this chapter. We don't expect you to get the answer correct. Hint: all the years have a different asset class answer.

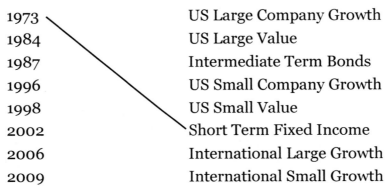

1973	US Large Company Growth
1984	US Large Value
1987	Intermediate Term Bonds
1996	US Small Company Growth
1998	US Small Value
2002	Short Term Fixed Income
2006	International Large Growth
2009	International Small Growth

Past performance is no guarantee of future results.

Nobody knows what asset class will be the best in any year until after the year is finished.

Therefore, you need to invest in *all* the various asset classes all the time, not just the ones that did well the year before! The one that did well last year often has the worst returns the following year. The way you control and manage your risks is by staying put once you are globally diversified. Yes, doing *nothing*, just stay in all the asset classes... forever, especially when your friends say and do otherwise! You want different investment results, so your behavior must be different.

Your portfolio may look different to any other Investors' portfolio, as you are continually diversified in the 20-plus different asset classes, each with a different level of risk.

Because the market is random, you need to always be in the broad global market, in order to capture the market returns. What are your returns expectations? Expect to receive market returns, after all, you own the market. If you assume you'll get better than market returns, you might have your expectations unmet. You need reasonable and appropriate investment expectations in order to have peace of mind. No one can predict the future, so it is best to be prudently globally diversified and stay the course over your lifetime in order to get market returns. Expect to get market returns, as only then will you have a successful investment experience!

Abe and Hatti thought they were appropriately diversified. They had 17 different mutual funds in 17 different investment companies. After all, their parents had told them not to put all their eggs in one basket, so, they had 17 separate investment baskets, but not much money invested into any of them. Their overlap analysis revealed their various money managers were duplicating many of the same stocks and bonds, their investment costs were excessive, their risks were twice as high as the level of risk they were comfortable with, plus, the worst news was that their investment returns were very low for the high risks they were taking.

Abe and Hatti just had more "stuff," all duplicating each other. In their case, more was not better! Duplicating assets makes your portfolio expensive and poorly diversified. As stated before, no one wants to buy Pepsi with six different money managers, some buying and some selling at the same time. Investors have no idea if their different retail mutual fund money managers are buying and selling the same stock at the same time within their portfolio until they see their portfolio's overlap analysis report. It is easy to eliminate duplicity of investments. Each of your mutual funds needs to purchase only one level of risk.

Most Investor portfolios are also missing at least half of the asset classes. We have never found a new Investor with a diversified portfolio for their risk tolerance style. Just like Abe and Hatti, typical Investors are under-diversified and taking on way too much risk for their peace of mind while receiving too small a return for the extra risk they are taking. Sadly, Investors don't have knowledge of their portfolio's risk until the results of their portfolio's investment analysis are completed. Unbelievable! How can you possibly manage risks you aren't even aware of?

Brinson, Singer, and Beebower in their 1996 "Determinants of Portfolio Performance II: An Update" research paper confirmed their earlier research that over 91% of your portfolio's performance, appreciation and growth, is dependent on asset allocation. This is very important so we'll say it again.

> *It is your portfolio's asset allocation, broad global diversification, that you must be most concerned about more than any other investment strategy or determinant: not stock picking, not market timing, not track record investing, and not costs, as over 91% of your portfolio's returns come from prudent diversification!*

The problem is, so many Investors' portfolios have inadequate asset diversification, and sadly, they have no clue there is a problem, especially the traders! Ignorance is not bliss; it hurts your future and your future descendants. Not knowing is not OK.

As you have already learned, individual stock picking has historically underperformed the S&P 500 Index returns and cannot give Investors prudent diversification, as individual stocks have minimal diversification. You would need thousands of individual stocks in multiple risk categories to become broadly diversified, so institutional stock and bond asset class mutual funds are the easiest way to accomplish this goal.

The type of mutual fund you invest in makes a big difference.

Retail mutual funds are typically no-load (no obvious commission), front-load (A shares), B shares (back-load), C shares (fixed commission per year), and other names... plus additional hidden mutual fund expenses such as actively traded funds are available through broker dealers and could have higher turnover and higher expenses.

The Free Market philosophy is available from Coaches and uses fee institutional asset class mutual funds, which typically have lower costs. Each institutional asset class mutual fund focuses on and buys only one level of risk, along with some cash for future purchases. That's right, just one asset class—level of risk—per mutual fund, and they buy all the stocks in that category that fit their parameters, and hold them... until that stock no longer fit that fund's parameters!

King Solomon wrote about diversification. He believed that the more diversified you were, the better the chance of surviving troubled times. He wrote that you should divide your assets up into at least seven to eight different area as life was like the wind, and those who do not rely on God have a meaningless life, as God is the center and creator of everything.

In his old age, King Solomon, the assumed writer of Ecclesiastes, reflected that we should be adventurous like those who accept the risks of trade and reap the rewards.

He also promotes not playing safe even though there were plenty of unseen dangers and that anyone can decide to change their life. Just start right where you are, as no one knows the future and life is short. We encourage you to take King Solomon's advice.

Cast your bread upon the waters, for after many days you will find it again. Give portions to seven, yes to eight, for you do not know what disaster may come upon the land. As you do not know the path of the wind, or how the body is formed in a mother's womb, so you cannot understand the work of God, the Maker of all things. Sow your seed in the morning, and at evening let not your hands be idle, for you do not know which will succeed, whether this or that, or whether both will do equally well. However many years a man may live, let him enjoy them all...

— Ecclesiastes 11:1-2, 5-6, 8

Asset Class Funds

Institutional asset class mutual funds differ from index funds. Both the asset class mutual funds and the index funds each include one category of risk, or asset class. However, by its own requirement, the index fund must buy and sell a portion of its specific asset class each year when updating its list of qualifying companies. Therefore, index mutual funds could have higher turnover rates than the institutional asset class mutual funds that own all the viable stocks in their asset classes. In addition, index funds only hold a portion of an asset class. Of the total approximately 3500 stocks listed as domestic large company stock, the S&P Index Fund only invests in 500.

Each institutional asset class mutual fund strives to keep at least 80% of its holdings within the same asset class matching its name, such as domestic large company stock asset class. Therefore, the domestic fund buys and holds domestic large company stocks, forever, unless one of the stocks changes classification or no longer fits the asset class fund's parameters. Then that stock can be moved to another more appropriate asset category.

Assume a Domestic Large Value company improves its position and becomes a Domestic Large Growth company asset. The Domestic Large Value asset class managers can move the upgraded stock from Domestic Large Value to Domestic Large Growth.

Where index funds might not be the right choice, also consider the problems with Exchange Traded Funds (ETFs). Many Investors believe Exchange Traded Funds are very similar and less expensive than index funds; however, these Investors have not looked closely and compared them to asset class mutual funds. The Exchange Traded Funds cannot give you the broad global diversification. In addition, the ETFs' costs lower your returns as expenses come out first before you receive profits.

Remember, we earlier showed you that your asset allocation— broad global diversification—is what explains over 91% of your portfolio's returns. Because the Free Market philosophy supports broad global diversification, your portfolio resembles a global market. Just stick with the institutional asset class mutual funds. It is common sense...simpler, uncomplicated, and usually cheaper!

As explained earlier, in Chapter 5 and to refresh your memory, to simplify the investing of multiple asset classes, the global market philosophy combines unique stock asset classes into two stock funds, domestic and international, and one bond fund, in which each holds the appropriate asset class mutual funds. These three funds are therefore called funds of funds.

As you also remember, in the last chapter we named these three mutual funds: domestic stock fund, international stock fund, and the bond fund. The domestic stock and international stock funds are made up of small, large, value, emerging markets and microcap stock asset class mutual funds. The bond fund of funds holds government, global, cash, two-year and five-year fixed income, money markets and treasuries asset class mutual funds. To have a prudently diversified portfolio, an Investor will own up to 20-plus of these different asset classes. Because the portfolio contains all or a good portion of these investment categories, it receives global market returns, as mentioned earlier—the majority of returns come from asset allocation! Don't worry, you don't have to do this, your money manager does it for you. Once your global diversified portfolio is created...it is only changed to rebalance back to its correlation targets. No more buying and selling when markets change! You just need to know why he is doing it so you have peace of mind.

Look ahead to your reward of an abundant stress-free investing experience, just like Moses had faith and suffered for his beliefs, you too will need to stand up for your Free Market beliefs. Your portfolio will always look different to your friends and peers, and they may not understand why you don't worry about the economy. Just look ahead to your reward of no more investor abuse or stress!

By faith Moses, when he had grown up, refused to be known as the son of Pharaoh's daughter. He chose to be mistreated along with the people of God rather than to enjoy the pleasures of sin for a short time. He regarded disgrace for the sake of Christ as of greater value than the treasures of Egypt, because he was looking ahead to his reward.

– Hebrews 11:24-26

Risk

Jack wanted to meet immediately! He was in a hurry, a self-imposed rush! He had just celebrated his 50th birthday and reality had finally sunk in. Jack finally realized that he didn't want to work until he died, so he had better start planning for his future retirement at 65. By now, you know we ask Investors for their goals and how they want to live their retirement lifestyle. Jack's only goal was to become a millionaire before he retired in 15 years. Now, it doesn't take an advanced mathematician to see that he had an unreasonable goal, especially once you know that Jack only had $100,000 in his retirement plan, a huge mortgage on his home, and no other savings. He and his wife were living paycheck to paycheck. Jack was dreaming the same fantasy that many other investors dream, desiring to get double digit rates of return with T-Bill type risks. In reality, what most investors get is exactly the opposite... T-Bill returns with greater market risks. Yes, Investors are periodically irrational, like Jack. He wanted no risk and more than a 10% return!

Jack started too late, and now it was virtually impossible to get him where he wanted to be within his timeframe. He definitely had to adjust his goals to be more reasonable and change his lifestyle in order to save for his retirement. Coaching is about saying "No" to unreasonable Investors and their behavior that is inappropriate for their goals. If an Investor desires a goal, he must be willing to walk his talk and be rational. We cannot be a part of helping an Investor fail. Successful Investors are patient and willing to take reasonable risks to get reasonable market returns in a reasonable timeframe.

Risk is usually described as a standard deviation number or the amount of volatility—movement on a risk scale. A good risk is one that can be managed and that will reasonably compensate the Investor over time, according to the level of volatility the Investor feels comfortable with. The level of risk—standard deviation numbers—typically goes from 0% (no risk) to 45% (very high risk). We personally have never seen a higher standard deviation number than 45%, but that doesn't mean there isn't any. The higher the risk, the more likely your investments will be volatile and potentially lose money. We'll use the term "risk" instead of standard deviation.

Never take the higher risk unless you are sure the investment you decide to participate in also gives you an extra return—called an investment premium—for taking the extra risk. The ideal situation is to receive the market return with a lower risk. To get a lower risk, manage the risk by having very broad diversification with unique dissimilar institutional asset class mutual funds. Statistically, the market goes up two years out of three, so you must always be in the market. Risk is necessary for growth, as there is no return without taking risk.

Every asset class has its own unique market cycle and volatility, or risk. The expected premium return from each asset class is determined by the amount of risk taken, its correlation, and its dissimilar cycle to other assets in the portfolio. Dissimilar cycles offset other asset class cycles. If your portfolio invests in only one level of risk, one asset class, your portfolio will have no diversification of market risk or dissimilar market cycles. Therefore, you'll experience greater risk, as your whole portfolio will respond in tandem. Buying all the companies with the same level of risk can be thought of as a single asset class, such as the S&P 500 US Large blend asset class, which has very limited diversification all by itself, and therefore has a greater risk than multiple dissimilar asset class portfolios. If you have more appropriate dissimilar asset classes in your portfolio you'll also have greater opportunities for better returns, or larger investment premiums. Remember, over 91% of your returns come from prudent diversification or dissimilar asset class cycles. You need multiple asset classes to be a stress-free successful investor.

Therefore, when you own all the viable stock of the businesses in the world you would have the greatest diversification possible and less risk, as you'll have multiple levels of risk in your portfolio. Investing in 12,000+ stocks and bonds in 40 plus different countries has a positive effect on the global economy and broadly spreads and lowers your market risk.

Globally diversified Free Market portfolios currently invest in over 40 countries and more are being added:

Argentina	Japan
Australia	Malaysia
Austria	Mexico
Belgium	Netherlands
Brazil	New Zealand
Canada	Norway
Chile	Philippines

China

Czech Republic

Denmark

Finland

France

Germany

Greece

Hong Kong

Hungary

India

Indonesia

Ireland

Israel

Italy

Poland

Portugal

Singapore

South Africa

South Korea

Spain

Sweden

Switzerland

Taiwan

Thailand

Turkey

United Kingdom

United States

While principal risk to some degree is unavoidable, many Investors make it worse on themselves because their diversification is too narrow for too long a time. Once you believe in the Free Market philosophy, your Coach will keep your portfolio in the Modern Portfolio Theory's broad diversification, multiple levels of dissimilar asset classes, which historically reduces your risk.

How does your current Advisor measure your portfolio's risk? If your portfolio's risk is not measured, how can it be controlled or managed? Most Investors have no idea how much risk they are taking, as their Advisor has never done a risk analysis.

Your biggest risk is not being in the market and not achieving your goals—your dreams! When you discuss your investment objectives and your Investment Philosophy (IP) with your Coach, make sure you discuss your written goals, and then focus on how to increase the probability of achieving these goals. God rewards faithfulness and perseverance. Focus on your goals and pleasing God (Job 42:10-12, Matthew 25: 14-30).

To read more about risks, please check our Book & DVD List for *The Successful Investor Today* by Swedroe and for Professor Malkiel's previously mentioned book.

Correlation

Correlation is a statistical measure of how two securities move in relation to each other and is used when building a portfolio. It is an essential ingredient of the Free Market philosophy, as dissimilar correlation helps your portfolio grow in a steady manner, cycling up and down on their own timelines. As an example, small companies are dissimilar to large companies; therefore, combining them reduces the volatility of your portfolio because their market cycles are unique from each other. The same is true for international stocks and domestic stocks. You need both in your portfolio. Due to the dissimilar market cycles of the different asset classes in the portfolio, the correlation of the portfolio will seek to obtain market returns with lower risk. Even though some levels of asset class are higher risk, the correlation of the whole is greater than the individual portfolio's parts, resulting in lower risk and higher returns.

Trillions of dollars were lost by growth Investors between 2000 and 2002 because they invested most of their money in similar investments, such as the S&P 500 Index asset class, which lost over 40%. It is simple... similar investments get similar results! Many Investors who lost so much money did not have lowly or un-correlated assets, as all their funds were in the same asset class.

Correlation and diversification work together in your portfolio for better returns. Correlation and rebalancing keep their portfolios appropriate for the Investors' risks. Many retail mutual fund investors' accounts had not even come back totally before the next 2008 soft market occurred.

You can control your risks and your costs, but you cannot control returns! Don't focus on returns! You need to focus on your costs and your risks. Free Market Investors are prudent risk takers as they have portfolios that are more broadly diversified than many other investment strategies. The greater the diversification and the better the correlation, the lower the risk and the more potential for steady returns. Returns come from taking prudent risks and being continuously in the market.

Staying disciplined, on the straight and narrow path produces a harvest of righteousness and peace. Although this is right for us it might not be a good fit for you. If this philosophy fits your needs, consider getting your portfolio prudently globally diversified into the Free Market philosophy and then stay the course!

No discipline seems pleasant at the time, but painful. Later on, however, it produces a harvest of righteousness and peace for those who have been trained by it.

– Hebrews 12:11

Three Factor Model

Along with MPT, staying disciplined in the various broad asset class categories and correlated for dissimilar risk levels within the portfolio, the Free Market efficient philosophy incorporates the Three Factor Model, developed by Eugene Fama and Kenneth French, some of the greatest minds in the current financial industry.

The Three Factor Model makes use of the latest academic knowledge to create and maintain a portfolio that suits your personal tolerance for risk and offers expected returns for lifelong success. Fama and French found that there are three dimensions of risk and return that must all be correlated within every portfolio.

The Three Factor Model portfolio *must haves* for both domestic and international assets are:

1. Market: Stocks vs. Bonds
2. Size: Large Companies vs. Small Companies
3. Value: Growth Companies vs. Value Companies

These three components, being in stocks instead of bonds, in small instead of large companies, in value instead of growth, support the best way to control your investment risk. Invest in a prudent global diversified portfolio that includes: domestic and international stocks; domestic and international bonds; domestic and international large companies; domestic and international small companies; domestic and international blended companies; domestic and international value companies; which is rebalanced religiously. Remember, international markets are great diversifiers for your portfolio. Don't be afraid of the international asset classes, embrace them! We learned earlier from Professor Malkiel's quote that there are huge differences in regional returns and that every portfolio should have substantial holdings in the emerging economies of the world... see quote earlier in this chapter.

What is your risk tolerance? Don't take the easy road and decide on a risk tolerance just like your spouse. Spouses are typically at different risk tolerances, so each individual needs to decide this for himself. If you decide to take control of your investments according to the Free Market, your Free Market Coach will help you select the right portfolio for your risk tolerance. Here are four of the seven standard portfolios we use. They all hold the unique institutional domestic, international, and bond asset class mutual funds, but in different percentages for each separate risk tolerance:

The Four Standard Portfolios:

1. Income: 25% Stocks & 75% Bonds
2. Balanced: 50% Stocks & 50% Bonds
3. Long-Term Growth: 75% Stocks & 25% Bonds
4. Aggressive: 95% Stocks & 5% Bonds

Many Investors use more than one portfolio risk tolerance for their individual accounts, according to how and when they plan to use each of their accounts. The rule of thumb is the longer the length of time you can wait to use your money, the more stock you can have in your portfolio, as *time is your friend*! Typically Roths and retirement plans for Investors younger than 35 are in a Aggressive Portfolio. Most Investors still receiving a paycheck, between the ages of 35 and 70, use a Long-Term Growth Portfolio. If you are living off your portfolio, you might want to use the Balanced Portfolio, so you can receive a 4%-5% steady income stream and have some additional growth of your portfolio. However, many senior citizens don't plan to use their Roths, but plan to use them for their children and grandchildren's inheritance, so they have invested their Roths in the Aggressive Portfolio. Everyone is unique, so decide your risk tolerance with your Coach.

Are you prudently invested? If not, you can change! If you aren't happy with the current way you are invested, you need to change to a more appropriate style of investing. Here is what King Solomon says about people who do not change when change is needed...

> *A prudent man sees danger and takes refuge, but the simple keep going and suffer for it.*
>
> *– Proverbs 22:3*

Step #3: Rebalance

Most Investors know this very important rule of investing: buy low and sell high, meaning buy equities when their price is low and sell once their value appreciates. Rebalancing follows the #1 rule of investing, "buy low and sell high." When you diversify into a globally diversified Free Market portfolio, your money manager will set a target percentage for each of the individual asset classes. The assets that outperform beyond their target need their gains sold off and reinvested into the target asset classes that underperformed. This process is called "rebalancing" and maintains appropriate portfolio weightings and offsets losses. Investors have a hard time doing the rebalancing for themselves, as money decisions are very emotional. Emotions lead many investors astray.

Rebalancing takes a tremendous amount of discipline and is difficult to do on your own. Have no worries, the money manager does this for you. He combines asset classes, both stocks and bonds, and rebalances them when they are "out of balance" back to their target percentages. Rebalancing can mean higher returns. Reread Professor Malkiel's quote in Chapter 5 #3... "Rebalancing improves your return by 1 and 1/3 percentage points per year." Disciplined design and rebalancing are necessary for successful investing results.

Polly and Doug came to the investment class at the local college and said every time they made a financial decision, the market crashed and they lost money! After listening and asking questions, we found that they were watching the market, and then as the market cycle crested, like a wave in the ocean, they invested, thereby buying every time at the market "high". No wonder they lost money, they disobeyed the first rule of investing, "buy low and sell high." Then Polly and Doug would get disgusted and sell, when the market was "low", in the valley of the wave. They were typical Investors making typical investor mistakes as they disobeyed the first rule of investing by doing the opposite: buying high and selling low! Because they didn't have a written Investment Philosophy (IP)—an investing road map—to follow, they were making common investment mistakes and then second-guessing themselves. They were... their own worst enemy!

Remember the large boat you visualized in the Retirement chapter, the one that we could all fit into and ride the ocean waves? Let's go back to that visualization however now let's use 4 boats. The Free Market philosophy is similar to everyone climbing into one of the four standard portfolio boats, along with other similar Investors. We all ride the market "waves" together, up and down, up and down. No one in each boat gets a better or worse return than the others in the same boat. As long as we all were in the same boat at the beginning of the trip and stay in the same boat without adding money or taking distributions, we all end up with similar returns, as we travel up and down, up and down, for our lifetime, our children's lifetime, and our beneficiaries lifetimes. If however someone changes boats or joins a boat during the trip, their returns would be different than those who stayed in for the whole ride, or left early.

As long as your money manager determines and sets targets for each asset class, and rebalances as needed, your risk tolerance portfolio should or has the potential to at least receive market returns, or might even do better than the market.

All the Investors in the same portfolio boat receive similar returns when they buy and hold, making the Free Market philosophy a WIN-WIN-WIN investment strategy! No one in the boat outperforms any of the others unless they got into the boat earlier than others got in or added additional money when the market was low! This Nobel Prize winning portfolio strategy gives you market returns no matter what the economy is doing. This means that you'll not always have the "best" returns each year, as an individual asset classes might temporarily do better than the whole market. Over your lifetime, you'll receive market returns commensurate with the risks you took. One of the benefits of the market "boat" is that we are riding the waves of the market together, allowing the market to adjust on its own.

All investing involves risk and costs. Our portfolios will also go down when the market goes down. No investment strategy, including asset allocation and diversification strategies, can guarantee peace of mind, assure profit, or protect against loss. There could be years where there is underperformance, however patience and maintaining discipline will reward you...eventually. Past performance is no guarantee of future performance.

> *It is better, if it is God's will,*
> *to suffer for doing good than for doing evil.*
>
> *– I Peter 3:17*

Step #4: Stop Moving Your Money... Forever!

Bert worked for one of the large Detroit automobile companies for many years, which had a retirement plan with some very expensive no-load investment options. Every Monday, Bert would check in with his office peers and then adjust his employer's retirement account, moving his investments according to what the market did the week before and what his peers projected the market would do in the future. His peers did the same.

Bert was his own worst enemy! He listened to his peers and moved his retirement money frequently. That was true... until he attended our Free Market classes. There he learned that each time you move your portfolio, your investment's highest risk cycle starts over again, the highest risk (of obtaining the historical expected return) time span being the first six years after each time his money moved. Each week Bert was actually starting a new 20-year risk vortex.

If your portfolio strategy needs a forecast to work, it is already flawed. Investors stay the course because over time, risk is reduced, expenses are reduced, and returns potentially increase due to lower costs. Fortunately, for our portfolios, rebalancing is usually accomplished with new Investors' influx of cash, so there is minimal buying and selling within existing accounts. After 20 years of holding the same portfolio, a prudent portfolio's market risk is almost eliminated.

Just listen to the good book, the Bible tells us to stay disciplined, build wealth slowly, over time. Be patient... and be wise.

He who ignores discipline comes to poverty and shame, but whoever heeds correction is honored. A longing fulfilled is sweet to the soul, but fools detest turning from evil. He who walks with the wise grows wise, but a companion of fools suffers harm.

— Proverbs 13:18-20

Free Markets work! The best way to create wealth is through continuously owning the global market. Money can make more money than you can make. Once your portfolio is properly diversified, ignore the feelings that you must do something when the market changes! Just hang on and enjoy your account value by staying disciplined and diversified in the market. While this world has no guarantees, history suggests that once prudently diversified, the less you move your money and the longer you hold it, the better your returns will be, as you'll no longer incur active trading expenses.

How did your long-term growth portfolio do during previous market crashes? Each of the past market crashes was unique and so was the rebound of the market after the crash. Learn from history! The market crash information is from the US Long-term bonds, bills, inflation, and fixed income factor data copyright "Stocks, Bonds, Bills, and Inflations Yearbook", Ibbotson Associates, Chicago, an annually updated work by Roger Ibbotson and Rex Sinquefield.

The buy-and-hold approach comparison uses a hypothetical 70% Stock/30% Bond domestic stock mix with seven different asset classes, as many of the small and international funds do not have a long audited history. Hypothetical Diversified 70/30 Portfolio indices being used: Long Term Government Bonds (15%), One Month US Treasury Bills (15%), Fama/French US Small Value Index (17%), Fama/French US Large Value Index (22%), CRSP Deciles 9-10 Index (11%), CRSP Deciles 6-10 Index (10%), S&P 500 Index (10%). Performance figures taken from DFA Returns Software Version: 2.0, 12/09.

The **Crash of 2008** lasted 16 months, October 2007 until February 2009. Investors with the buy-and-hold hypothetical growth portfolio lost -30.70%. However, by staying in the prudently diversified portfolio, their recovery took approximately 13 months, from April 2009 to April 2010, and they enjoyed an annualized one-year return of 57.28%.

The **Dot.Com** crash lasted 22 months, February 2001 until February 2003. Investors with a growth portfolio lost -36.40%, but by staying disciplined in a prudently diversified portfolio, their return one year after the crash was a positive 44.54%. In three years, their annualized return was 20.08%, and the five-year annualized return was 12.76%.

The 1987 Crash was only two months long, September to October 1987, with Investors losing -23.25%. After the 1987 crash, the prudently diversified Investor received a one-year 19.40% annualized return, a three-year annualized return of 6.07%, a five-year annualized return of 12.55%, a ten-year annualized return of 14.24%, and a 20-year annualized return of 11.80%.

The **Great Depression Crash** lasted 34 months, September 1929 to June 1932, resulting in a total portfolio return of -83.41%. No one knew about Free Markets during the Great Depression, but if they did, the numbers would have looked like this: Investors who maintained the hypothetical buy-and-hold long-term growth portfolio after the crash had a one-year Annualized Return of 257.00%, a three-year Annualized Return of 46.00%, a five-year Annualized Return of 43.03%, a 10-year Annualized Return of 17.40%, and a 20-year Annualized Return of 17.76%.

All it took to obtain these hypothetical returns after the market crashed was to be prudently and broadly diversified and then do *nothing*. Investors just needed to stay disciplined in the Nobel Prize winning academic investment strategy, Modern Portfolio Theory (MPT) and the Three Factor Model, while also diversifying and rebalancing!

Past performance is not indicative of future performance. All investing involves risks and costs. Your Advisor can provide you with more information about the risks and costs associated with specific programs. No investment strategy (including asset allocation and diversification strategies) can ensure peace of mind, assure profit, or protect against loss.

Apply your heart to instruction and your ears to words of knowledge. My son, if your heart is wise, then my heart will be glad; My inmost being will rejoice when your lips speak what is right.

– Proverbs 23:12, 15-16

Save Your Money & Gain Free Time

Stop spending your hard-earned money on things you no longer need, want, or desire. We have strived to reduce investing to its simplest level...simplified investing. Applying your new knowledge, not spending money, brings pleasant riches and contentment. Many times it is what you don't do that is truly best for your lifestyle.

If you decide to commit to the wisdom of the Free Market philosophy, you'll stop doing things that do not support your financial well-being and your long-term goals. Stop losing money and feeding the scam artists. Stop paying for reports and information you no longer need, as you no longer need these "noisy" intrusions into your life. Because of your new beliefs, you'll no longer feel it necessary to watch the financial media or buy financial newspapers, trading newsletters, stock-picking books, and financial magazines that talk about the next hot stock picks or what the top best stocks were last year.

Just these few changes will reward you with lower investment costs, lower taxes, dissolve financial confusion, eliminate stressful feelings that you are out of the financial "loop," and you'll no longer experience information overload.

Adding up all the money you'll save by *not* buying two $5 financial magazines a month saves you $120 a year! Now, add your costs of *not* buying any financial newspapers, approximately $100 a year, and you are up to $220 in savings, simply by *not* reading about what everyone is guessing about... the future market movements and old historical information. Did you also cancel your trading newsletters, a saving of about $200 a year... so now you are saving at least $440! Never again will you feel the guilt that you need to read everything and anything about the market and think you are missing out on important market information. If you want information overload to be a thing of the past, change your investment philosophy. It is up to you. If you answer "Yes," it is *done*! Never again to be repeated. You are a stress-free and efficient Investor heading down the successful abundant Investor path.

Look at all the time you are saving by not reading the financial newspapers, letters, and magazines! Free Market Investors can gain up to 12 hours a week just by *not* reading hard copy or online financial media opinions. Now you can also avoid listening to radio and watching TV shows about stock picking, market timing, and track record investing—more time saved for other more interesting activities.

No one knows the future any more than you do. You have heard the saying that if there are 12 economists in the room, there will be 13 opinions. Everyone is guessing at future market movements. You can learn from the past but you cannot predict the future by looking at the past. Only God knows the future, so don't waste your precious time!

Congratulations, you are in the process of learning the *truths* of investing. Bottom line, active trading is a scandal, and you are the victim.

We see a huge problem. Most Advisors have no idea about Free Markets or how they work. The sad *truth* is that many aren't even considering helping their Investors by searching for a better way to invest. If Advisors aren't even searching for a better way to help Investors, how can they possibly find it? Yes, many Advisors have heard about Modern Portfolio Theory (MPT) and believe they are actually providing it to their Investors. In reality, they are listening to their broker dealers and trying to accomplish it with poorly diversified retail mutual funds. That doesn't work. Also, they don't realize that MPT is only one component of the Free Market philosophy. Therefore, in order for you to move to this philosophy, you must learn more about your current Advisor.

In the next chapter, we'll give advice about talking to your current Advisor. We have a list of questions for you to use when talking to him so you can see if he is able to help you invest in the Free Market strategies. If he cannot answer these questions, and you feel this philosophy fits your needs, you'll then need to move on to a different Advisor, a Free Market Coach. We also give you questions to help you find this Coach.

Is it time to gain your freedom from financial abuse and lack of knowledge? We have educated you on the simplified *truths* of investing, so now it is time for you to cut through the hype and overcome the barrage of information from the financial industry and the media. It is time for you to reclaim your peace of mind. It is time to step out of your comfort zone and take the next step of faith by following your heart.

Aim for perfection, listen to my appeal, be of one mind, live in peace. And the God of love and peace will be with you.
— *2 Corinthians 13:11*

Free Market Investors Speak Out

We have all gone through some tough markets. However, our Investors may not have suffered the huge losses like active market Investors. Also, they have most likely recouped their smaller losses quicker than active market Investors just by staying disciplined and doing nothing once prudently diversified.

Here is what our Investors tell their loved ones, family, friends and coworkers when they are asked about their investment strategy and why they aren't worried during the tough times:

1. I am in the best investment position possible! I own over 12,000-plus different global stocks and bonds in 20-plus different domestic and international asset classes.

2. I believe in buying low and selling high, and that is exactly what my money manager's periodic rebalancing does.

3. I have the best possible diversification, as I own the a large portion of the global market, investments from 40 plus free countries! When a domestic or international company does well, I already own it! In addition, my money manager allocates them all for me, automatically.

4. Yes, the market goes down. However, because I already own a large portion of the global market, when it goes back up, I should capture the gain.

5. My focus is on the long-term results of the market, not the short-term sector returns. Over time, markets have always recovered and gone up. I ignore market movements.

6. I am better diversified and have less investment cost now that I'm invested in a buy and hold globally diversified investment philosophy.

7. Love the simplicity and I no longer need complex investments. I no longer feel that I have to change my portfolio when the market changes.

8. Simple tools to improve my stewardship.

9. I no longer have doubts or worries about my personal stewardship.

10. Investing is really about common sense.

> *Do not merely listen to the word, and so deceive yourselves. Do what it says...*
>
> *– James 1:22*

So now you see, there is another way to invest. You may feel it's time to stop gambling and speculating with your hard-earned money. You need *true* diversification, an investment strategy that has fewer expenses. By moving to Free Markets, you'll reduce commissions, eliminate surrender penalties, reduce market stress, eliminate stock picking, avoid information overload, and avoid confusion.

This change can help you achieve financial peace of mind, as you'll not be purchasing products from the scandal-ridden investment companies that are constantly being written about in the news. The money they use to commit these scandals comes from you, their Investors.

You have now learned how simple it is to be a successful stress-free Investor, and how important it is to fulfill your God-given purpose and pass on your wisdom and virtues to your heirs.

Knowing what you want God's money to do for you and what you want to achieve in life makes your future financial decisions so much easier.

No longer will you do stock selection and market timing, as long as you walk your talk and desire eternal security, happiness and peace of mind.

Are you ready to make a change and focus on a lifetime of eternal peace of mind? Are you ready to forget the past and take control of your future? Investors with as little as $100 a month can enjoy the rewards of Free Market.

> *...forgetting what is behind and straining*
> *toward what is ahead...*
>
> *– Philippians 3:13*

Your Decision Time

It is time to make your Free Market philosophy decision. Not making a change is a decision to continue getting the results you currently get. What happens if you do *nothing... <u>read it again...</u> NOTHING*! If you want different results, you must have different beliefs, followed by different behaviors.

The next chapter gives you three sets of questions for you to use, the first is a summary for yourself, and the next two are to help you find and hire the right Coach for you and your family.

Best Performing Asset Class Exercise Answers

1973	Short Term Fixed Income
1984	US Large Value
1987	International Small Growth
1996	US Small Value
1998	US Large Company Growth
2002	Intermediate Term Bonds
2006	International Large Growth
2009	US Small Company Growth

Past Performance is not a guarantee of future results. The Value of Diversification and Asset Classes with Low Correlation Based on the Best and Worst Performing Asset

Source: 37 Year performance figures taken from Dimensional Fund Advisors (DFA) Returns software 12/09. Some data provided to DFA by the Center for Research & Security Pricing (CRSP), University of Chicago. US Large Company stocks are represented by the S&P 500 Index; US Large Value stocks are represented by Fama / French US Large Value Research Index; US Small Company stocks are represented by CRSP 9-10 Index; US Small Value stocks are represented by Fama / French US Small Value Research Index; International Large stocks are represented by MSCI EAFE Index (Gross Div.); International

Small stocks are represented by International Small Company Index; Intermediate Term Bonds are represented by Long Term Government Bond Index; Short Term Fixed Income is represented by DFA One Year Fixed Income Portfolio; and Cash is represented by One Month T-Bills. This material has been obtain from sources generally considered to be reliable. No guarantee can be made to its accuracy. Not intended to represent the performance of any particular investment. Indices are unmanaged and on cannot invest directly in an index.

All investing involves risk and costs. No investment strategy (including asset allocation and diversification strategies) can ensure peace of mind, assure profit, or protect against loss.

Submit to God and be at peace with him; in this way prosperity will come to you. Accept instruction from his mouth and lay up his words in your heart.

– Job 22:21-22

7

Interview Your Advisor!

How much better to get wisdom than gold, to choose
understanding rather than silver!

— Proverbs 16:16

Know Your Advocate

Your financial Advisor is your advocate and guardian. What do you really know about your current Advisor? An advocate seeks to provide you with the best available and as protect you as a guardian. Do you have the best investments, in good times and bad times, no matter what the economy? Now that you realize there is a simpler stress-free way to invest, it's time to start your journey to obtain your own financial peace of mind. Many women readers have taken care of others for years. Now it is time to take care of yourself and your future well-being. We want you to have an enviable lifestyle.

The first step is to learn more about your current Advisor. How well do you know him? How proactive is he? Has your Advisor communicated frequently with you during the storm of the last severe market downturns and kept you from the depths of losses? He is supposed to be your advocate and guardian.

Before you decide to stay with your current Advisor or to hire a new Free Market Coach, you must learn more about how they work, their investment philosophy, and their investment process. Then you also need to find out what strategies they use to implement their philosophies. The questions in this chapter will help you.

Sadly, many Advisors say they invest using the Modern Portfolio Theory (MPT) strategy to create a Free Market portfolio. However, when you hold them accountable, their behavior doesn't match their talk. They still use expensive and overlapping retail-commission and no-load mutual funds that include 12b-1 costs, C shares, B shares, and some no-load funds. Some even have penalties or surrender charges to leave early. That's correct, some no-load funds have penalties! No-load does not necessarily mean inexpensive!

By this time, you know it is impossible for commission or no-load Advisors to offer the Free Market philosophy. These strategies however can be accomplished through the fee Advisory process and institutional asset class mutual funds, while also incorporating the Three Factor Model. The stress-free type funds are only available from fee Free Market Coaches who are Investment Advisory Representative of Registered Investment Advisors. They do not receive any commissions, incentives, free trips, or other benefits before or after the funds are bought or sold. Having read Chapter 3, about avoiding investment abuses, you also know you must only work with an Advisor who walks his talk. Yes, it is true for everyone... actions speak louder than words! So, before you decide to move to a Free Market Coach, talk to your current Advisor and get the answers straight from him. You need to ask challenging questions.

Start by asking yourself this question, "What have I learned from my Advisor this past year?" Do you have Free Market educational sessions offered to you to help you understand how the market works? If he doesn't take the time to educate you, you have to wonder why. Could it be he doesn't want you to know what he knows? You have a life and are focused on your life, so you depend on your financial advocate to help you understand this very important part of your life.

Also, listen to an Advisor who has experienced multiple tough markets and has helped Investors avoid severe losses during down markets by managing their risks. It isn't until an Advisor has lived through the hard times that he realizes how important your risk tolerance and your understanding of the market is. You also don't want an Advisor who agrees with you all the time. You want someone who will tell you the *truth*, even if it goes against your desires. You need someone who has integrity, honesty, good character and is willing to be vulnerable.

> *Buy the truth and do not sell it; get wisdom,*
> *discipline and understanding.*
>
> *– Proverbs 23:23*

Your Free Market Review

Before you interview an Advisor, make sure you first understand these questions and answers. They are a review of the previous chapters.

Once you have your Coach, to fully understand the knowledge you need for financial peace of mind, complete all the classes your Coach offers. Peace of mind comes through knowledge of the *truths* of investing.

> *Preservation of capital is very important.*
> *Does your current Investment Philosophy approach*
> *this concern?*

Your Investment Philosophy is a statement of your investment beliefs and strategies, your road map for risk taking, fulfilling your dreams, and staying ahead of inflation. Without it, your investment decisions will be "pot luck." With it, the decisions are easy. Just like Fortune 500 companies, everyone needs an investment plan and needs to work their plan. Coaching helps you develop your road map for risk, your Investment Philosophy.

185

> ### *Is the composition of your current portfolio consistent with your Investment Philosophy? How have you confirmed that your portfolio is and remains truly diversified?*

Investment analyses show that many retail money managers do not invest according to the mutual fund's stated objectives. Many value mutual funds are found to be heavily weighted in growth S&P 500 stocks and some global funds are found to mostly invest in domestic S&P 500 stocks.

Safety in investing comes from staying ahead of inflation with prudent global diversification. Smart Investors use fee asset class mutual funds managed by institutional money managers, who keep their internal fees very low.

> ### *How are you measuring and controlling your portfolio risks?*

There are many types of risks, and not all risks are equally weighted: market, standard deviation, and diversification risk. Without measuring risk, there is no way to control your risks. By having an investment analysis and an overlap analysis completed on your existing portfolio, your risk can be measured. Only then will you be able to see the level of risk in your portfolio and then you can decide if you are comfortable with it.

> ### *What are the "True Costs" of your investments?*

Investment costs analyses have discovered that most annuities and mutual funds have high turnover rates; therefore, have very high hidden costs. From our costs analysis experiences, some expenses are 6% or higher a year, which the fund and annuity need to pay before the Investors enjoy any investment return. How efficient are your funds? What is your portfolio's turnover rate? Look in your mutual fund's prospectus to find some of these answers.

Are you open to cutting your expenses by approximately 30%-50%?

If your growth mutual funds have annual turnover rates over 20%, you are definitely paying excessive expenses. Large institutional asset class money managers have very low turnover rates. Therefore, their total expenses can be 30%-50% less than the typical no-load and retail-commission mutual funds that hold multiple asset classes within each fund. Income asset class mutual funds might have higher turnovers as they invest for short maturities.

The investment analysis and overlap analysis show that most retail mutual funds and retail annuities purchase the same investments. So if you own both, you are paying the same hidden costs multiple times over for duplicate investments. How many times do you want to pay different annuity and mutual fund's buy/sell spread costs on the same stocks?

Would you prefer market returns with less risk and less cost?

Most Investors do not know they have a choice of investment beliefs or strategies on how to invest. Once you determine your Investment Philosophy, your future investment decisions may be easier to make.

The Modern Portfolio Theory is a Nobel Prize winning academic strategy that has consistently given Investors better diversification and market returns with less risk and less cost.

Yes, the words all Americans like to hear... better and cheaper!

Now that you have gone through the summary above, make a copy of the following questions to use during your interview(s). Remember to write down the answers you receive so you have a hard copy and don't have to depend on your memory.

> *Blessed is the man who finds wisdom, the man who gains understanding, for she is more profitable than silver and yields better returns than gold. She is more precious than rubies; nothing you desire can compare with her. Long life is in her right hand; in her left hand are riches and honor. Her ways are pleasant ways, and all her paths are peace. She is a tree of life to those who embrace her; those who lay hold of her will be blessed.*
>
> *— Proverbs 3:13-18*

Ask Your Current Advisor

Here are some pertinent questions to ask your current Advisor. If you don't currently have an Advisor or decide to change Advisors, skip this list and move on to the second list to interview and find a Free Market Coach.

You might also want to do a random act of kindness. Your current Advisor might be looking for a better way to invest, as it took us 18 years to find the Free Market philosophy, so tell him about this alternative philosophy.

The Free Market (FM) answers you want to hear are in the parentheses. To save time and energy, you might want to contact your current Advisor on the phone and ask the questions—start at the top and work down. If you get through two questions and neither answer is close to the answer we have provided, politely excuse yourself and thank the Advisor for his time. You are wasting your valuable time asking any more questions.

If your Advisor gets the answers all correct, ask him why he hasn't told you this information before, and then if you are satisfied with the answer, ask for an appointment to move 100% of your portfolio to the global Free Market philosophy as soon as possible. Time is of the essence! Nobody knows God's timing or His plans... so keep moving forward.

1. **Who does my portfolio's quarterly rebalancing?**

   (FM Answer: Your money manager)

2. **What is the turnover of each of my growth mutual funds?**

   (FM Answer: Below 20% per year—anything higher is too expensive)

3. **How are you held accountable for making sure my different mutual funds don't duplicate stocks or bonds?**

   (FM Answer: By using only funds that purchase institutional asset class mutual funds)

4. **How do you measure and control my portfolio's risk?**

   (FM Answer: Your risks are measured by the investment analysis. Your risks are controlled by keeping your funds invested only in the efficient institutional domestic and international asset class mutual funds, and applying both the Modern Portfolio Theory diversification and the Three Factor Model to your portfolio.)

5. **How *truly* diversified is my current portfolio?**

a. How many unique stocks and bonds do I own and how do I own them?

   (FM Answer: You own composite funds that hold asset class funds which have over 12,000-plus unique stocks and bonds)

b. How many countries am I invested in?

(FM Answer: 40 plus different free countries)

c. How many different asset classes am I invested in? (FM Answer: 20-plus different asset class categories)

6. Is my portfolio completely liquid or do I have penalties and surrender charges?

(FM Answer: Our portfolios are 100% liquid. They don't have front or back loads and never any penalties or surrender charges.)

7. How can my investment costs become tax deductible?

(FM Answer: Advisory fees can be deducted annually on your 1040's Miscellaneous Itemized Deductions. Your Coach will send you an accounting of your fees at the end of each year.)

8. How are you paid and what did you earn off my accounts last year?

(FM Answer: Advisory fees are reported on your portfolio's quarterly statements. You have three levels of fees, 1). Advisory fee, 2). Funds Fees, and 3). Institutional Asset Class Mutual Fund fees. All fees total about 2% or less.)

An honest answer is like a kiss on the lips.

– Proverbs 24:26

Finding a Free Market Coach

Use this list of questions to find and interview a Free Market Coach. Again, the answers you want to hear are in parentheses. If you are unable to find a Coach, talk to the person who gave you this book, or go to our website to help locate a Free Market Coach:

www.Stress-FreeInvesting.com

Save time by calling and telling the person who answers the phone that you would like to talk to the Free Market Coach. If the reply you receive isn't clear, the Advisor in this office doesn't know how to invest according to the Free Markets Portfolio Theory. Thank the receptionist for her time and call the next Advisor on your list. Your time is too valuable to talk to the wrong Advisor.

1. **Are you a fee only, fee-based, or commission-based Advisor?**
   (FM Answer: "Fee-only" means the Advisor is paid only by Advisory fees. Fee-based means the Advisor receives mostly fees and some commissions—typically from insurance products. Commission-based Advisors are paid mostly by commissions but might have some fees, typically from C share mutual funds. You want an Advisor who is fee-only or fee-based.)

2. **How do you keep my portfolio composition *true* to my investment philosophy?**
   (FM Answer: First we see what your investment beliefs are, then we use investment strategies that are consistent with your beliefs.)

3. **What is the turnover rate of each *growth* mutual fund or annuity you are suggesting I invest in?**
   (FM Answer: 20% or less per year, anything higher is actively managed and too expensive.)

4. **What are the total annual expenses for each**

mutual fund or variable annuity investment you are suggesting?

(FM Answer: Total investment costs vary according to risk level, all three fee levels (Advisory, Funds, and Asset Class are typically 2.6% or lower per year.)

5. **How do you measure and control investment risk?**

(FM Answer: The investment analysis measures your portfolios' volatility, and risk. Risk is controlled with the Modern Portfolio Theory and the Three Factor Model, which use prudent global diversification, minimum trading, and low investment costs.)

6. **Can I claim my investment costs on my 1040 tax return?**

(FM Answer: Yes, all Advisory fees on taxable accounts, or fees paid outside of tax-deferred or tax-free accounts, are miscellaneous itemized deductions on your 1040.)

7. **Will you be able to tell me where my portfolio fits on the Nobel Prize winner Harry Markowitz' Efficient Frontier?**

(FM Answer: This will be revealed in the investment analysis report, as it reveals the intersection of your current portfolio's risk and return.)

8. **How do you make sure that all my stocks and bonds are 100% liquid, unique and not duplicated?**

(FM Answer: Our portfolios never have front loads, back loads, surrender charges or penalties. They are always 100% liquid. The portfolios hold only institutional asset class mutual funds, which are all unique.)

9. Are you a Coach or a Financial Planner?

(FM Answer: We are Coaches, as we build a lifestyle relationship with you and help you make the important financial decisions throughout all of your life stages. One goal of a Coach is to help investors stay disciplined during trying markets and to teach them how not to hurt themselves by reacting to the media or by making common investing mistakes.)

Listen closely as the Advisors you are interviewing answer. Watch their body language and write down their answers. You want an Advisor who understands Free Markets and has already obtained peace of mind. Only then can he communicate ways to help you—the Investor.

Once you have found your Coach, and if you really want to invest stress-free, we encourage you to move your whole portfolio to this philosophy. You need to take care of yourself and your family... *now!* Tomorrow is not certain. Moving your money into the Free Market philosophy should be your #1 priority. We pray you have an abundant and enviable lifestyle. God bless you!

So do not throw away your confidence;
it will be richly rewarded. You need to persevere so that
when you have done the will of God, you will
receive what he has promised.
– Hebrews 10:35-36

Do you have investing concerns?

Let us help you become a successful investor and discover *your* peace of mind!

616-460-6518

www.Stress-FreeInvesting.com
www.WordhouseWealthCoaching.com
info@WordhouseWealthCoaching.com

If God is for us,
who can be against us?
– Romans 8:31

Book & DVD List

Beginning Investors:

Clason, George S. – *The Richest Man in Babylon*

Edwards, Samuel P. – *Remember the Vine, How to Grow Rich and Stay Rich*

Hill, Napoleon – *Think & Grow Rich*

Murray, Nick – *Simple Wealth, Inevitable Wealth*

Current Investors:

Acton Media – *The Call of the Entrepreneur* DVD

Alcorn, Randy – *Money, Possessions & Eternity*

Anderson, Dr. C. Thomas – *Becoming a Millionaire God's Way*

Blue with White – *The New Master Your Money*

Ellis, Charles D. – *Investment Policy, How to Win the Loser's Game*

George, Elizabeth – *The Remarkable Women of the Bible*

Hazlitt, Harry – *Economics in One Lesson*

Malkiel, Burton G. – A *Random Walk Down Wall Street*

Matson, Mark E. – *Flashpoint, Mastering the Art of Economic Abundance*

Swedroe, Larry E. – *The Successful Investor Today: 14 Simple Truths You Must Know When You Invest*

Taylor, Jill Bolte – *My Stroke of Insight*

Greed & Corruption:

Eichenwald, Kurt – *Serpent On The Rock*

Eichenwald, Kurt – *The Informant*

McLean & Elkind – *The Smartest Guys In The Room*

Reingold with Reingold, Dan – *Confessions of a Wall Street Analyst: A True Story of Inside Information and Corruption in the Stock Market*

Stoneman and Schulz – *Brokerage Fraud; What Wall Street Doesn't Want You to Know*

About the Authors

Phyllis and Maria are a mother-daughter Wealth & Stewardship Coaching team.

Phyllis J. Veltman Wordhouse is a registered Investment Advisory Representative, the founder of Wealth Advisors Group, LLC a Michigan Registered Investment Advisor and since 1982, the CEO of Wordhouse Wealth Coaching (WWC). Her professional expertise is in Wealth and Stewardship Coaching, especially to mature Christian women. Her mission is to teach Investors how to protect themselves from investment abuse and create scripturally based peace of mind.

Ms. Wordhouse' True Purpose for Life is to be Christlike. Ms. Wordhouse earned her BA degree in Education at Calvin College and Masters at Eastern Michigan University. She is a Qualified Member of Kingdom Advisors Network and a Certified Financial Planner. Ms. Wordhouse is a Certified Investor Coach and is a founding member of The Stewardship Alliance, a national Christian focus group of Wealth & Stewardship Coaches. Ms. Wordhouse also belongs to the International Association of Advisors in Philanthropy.

Ms. Wordhouse is happily married to Jerry Wordhouse, a retired successful commercial glass and glazing business owner. They have four adult children and ten beautiful grandchildren.

Maria J. Wordhouse Kuitula is a registered Investment Advisory Representative, the President of Wordhouse Wealth Coaching (WWC) and the Managing Member of Wealth Advisors Group (WAG), a Michigan Registered Investment Advisor firm. Ms. Kuitula has authored and co-authored several media published Wealth Coaching articles. She utilizes the

Nobel Prize winning Modern Portfolio Theory within the Free Market Portfolio Theory, which creates peace of mind and successful investor experiences. She helps investors align their *true* purpose for life with their spending and investing decisions.

Since 2000, Ms. Kuitula has been instrumental in helping WWC become more efficient, virtual, and paperless. Maria is a Qualified Member of the Kingdom Advisors Network (KA) and a member and volunteer for The Stewardship Alliance (TSA), a national Christian Wealth & Stewardship Coaching organization. She is also a member of the Life Stewardship Institute, which works with several financial experts to get to the heart of her Investors and develop financial strategies to accomplish their stewardship goals.

Ms. Kuitula has a Bachelor of Science Degree in Biomedical Photography from Rochester Institute of Technology. She moved to Grand Rapids, Michigan and married Don Kuitula her college sweetheart. They have two wonderful, active children, Mason and Sylvia. After working in ophthalmic photography for 10 years, Maria is following in Phyllis' footsteps educating Investors about the *truths* and lies of investing. Maria is the youngest daughter of Phyllis and Jerry Wordhouse.

Maria's True Purpose for Life is to honor and respect all of God's creation.

Acknowledgements

Without these people there would be no book, we owe you much sincere thanks and appreciation to:

First of all, our Investors, who so patiently joined and traveled with us on our journey! They continuously encouraged us for 18 years and gladly moved with trust and good humor to and from eight different broker dealers so we could eventually find the right investment philosophy that fit our virtues and beliefs. Your gracious patience during our search for the *truths* of investing will certainly be eternally rewarded in glory! Thank you for your stories, so others could learn from them. Without you, we would have been alone in our search and there would be no book. We appreciate you!

Our proofreaders! Our loving husbands, Don Kuitula and Jerry Wordhouse who patiently lived this journey with us by proofreading and re-proofreading the manuscript as we made changes. In addition, our faithful staff, Deb Ames and Debbie Tinkler, along with Debbie's husband, Mike Tinkler who also supported us through this writing process. We appreciate your unwavering belief in our project and wanting us to tell our story. Thank you for your hugs and unfaltering encouragement.

The Matson Money team, Mark Matson, Dan List, Zack Shepard, Steve Miller, Michelle Matson, and everyone who researched details for us and proofread the manuscript to make sure we were Free Market Portfolio Theory appropriate. Thanks for your constant encouragement to write a book. We appreciate your patient support and technical guidance. You are the best we have ever worked with!

We have received wonderful support and help from our

patient and supportive editor Mark Hooper. Thank you so much for giving us guidance, and helping us tell our story effectively, thereby making our book easier to read and understand.

Special thanks goes to our wonderful book reviewers for their candor and encouraging comments: Scott Preissler, Ph.D. Eklund Professor of Steward Leadership and Director of The Center for Steward Leadership Southwestern Baptist Theological Seminary; Mike B., Investor; Dr. John Brunstetter, CEO Team Interplay LLC; Pamela Otten, Radio Show Host of Intelligent Investing with Pamela Otten, The Financial Mom; Ray Slager, Professor of Accounting Emeritus, Greater West Michigan area; and Gregory W. Baker, J.D., ChFC®, CFP®, CAP, President, Renaissance Charitable Foundation Inc.

Andrea and Ross Wordhouse, Phyllis' daughter-in-law and son, who were instrumental with the design of the book cover, websites, and marketing support. Thank you so much for your continual design and marketing professional expertise and guidance!

Phyllis' other children, Heidi, Erik, Michelle and grandchildren, Rachael, Damian, Paige, Debbie, Xander, Mason, Wyatt, Sylvia, Seth, and Trevor. They were quiet while we wrote, supported and cheered us on so we could help other Investors, and celebrated with us during the journey, as they knew this was our passion. Thank you for all your hugs and loves! This book was written so other families could be as happy as you. Your love for us made this possible!

Lastly and most importantly, in memoriam, Phyllis and Jerry's parents: Rev. Nelson and Lois Veltman and Gerard Sr. and Martha Wordhouse. Thank you for giving us life and bringing us up with your Christian beliefs. For without them, we would not be saved and looking forward to spending our eternal reward with God and you, our loved ones. Neither of our parents had Free Market financial knowledge; however, they had the basis of all *truths*, the Bible, and they persevered in His

Word, as all financial decisions are scriptural.

We pray that your life is changed for the better through this book—our passion. Continue to be curious, live in peace and please your Creator. God bless you and your family!

Choose my instruction instead of silver, knowledge rather than choice gold, for wisdom is more precious than rubies, and nothing you desire can compare with her.

I, wisdom, dwell together with prudence; I possess knowledge and discretion.

— Proverbs 8: 10-12

Glossary

12b-1 Trails

A quarterly fee charged by some mutual funds to cover promotion, distribution, and marketing expenses paid to brokers and paid to your Advisor in lieu of or in addition to a Front or Back-Load commission in A and B and C Share mutual funds. Some no-load funds also charge 12b-1 fees. All fee information is disclosed in a mutual fund's prospectus.

Abundant Mentality

The abundant thinking person takes action and is committed to creating not only wealth but also peace of mind.

Active Markets

Proponents believe in market predictions, and therefore use stock picking, market timing and track record investing strategies. We believe this is gambling and speculating.

Adjusted Gross Income (AGI)

The bottom number on your 1040's first page, which totals all your various incomes minus any deductions.

Advisory Fee

A tax-deductible expense for investment advice and portfolio management charged by investment advisors.

Analyst

A highly paid person who suggests to stock brokers what to sell to the Investors. His or her predictions have been shown not to be any better than random luck.

Assets

What you own—typically, fund shares of an investment company. The investment company owns the stocks and bonds in mutual funds. Your house and car are also assets, but they are called "use assets" as you use them for your lifestyle and must not count them for retirement income.

Asset Class Mutual Funds

Mutual funds that own all the viable stocks and bonds in one level of risk, one asset category, and all its sectors. Each asset class mutual fund is named for the asset class it holds and is passively managed.

Back Load

Mutual funds or other investment that have a surrender charge if you desire to exit the investment before a certain time span, typically six years for "B" shares and one year for "C" shares.

Bear Markets

A prolonged period when the stock market share values go down, or are called "soft."

Bid/Ask Spread

Difference in price between the buy and sell prices and what the market maker on Wall Street is paid.

Broker Dealer

The company the Advisor works for and shares his commissions.

Bull Markets

A prolonged period when the stock market prices go up in value.

Commissions

What you pay when you use a broker dealer to buy or sell a security.

C Share Mutual Funds

Mutual funds with no upfront sales charge and a quarterly fee charged by the mutual fund with a portion paid to the broker dealer and your Advisor. Higher annual fees are charged against the fund for as long as the investor holds it. Shares have a lower back-end load than B shares and are chargeable against redemptions for a shorter period of time, usually a year. Some Advisors incorrectly believe these are fee investments.

Conflict of Interest

When the person who is making the decision receives a benefit from the decision, which may undermine that person's impartiality.

Control

When you can make your own decisions and know you have done the right things right.

Correlation

When your money manager sets and maintains a target percentage of each separate institutional asset class category within your portfolio.

Cost Basis

The total costs of an investment. In your portfolio, it would be all the contributions to your investments plus all reinvested dividends and interest.

Custodian

Your investment accountant. It reports to you every time any money moves in or out of your portfolio and keeps the IRS happy by doing all the necessary IRS compliance and reporting. Your custodian holds the assets in your accounts.

Delays

Time wasted while the broker waits to execute the trade.

Dissimilar Market Cycle

All asset classes have their own market cycles, when they go up in value and when they go down in value. The asset classes with market cycles that are least alike are called "dissimilar."

Diversification

In an investment portfolio, prudent diversification means the portfolio holds mostly "unique" global stocks and bonds, assets that have limited duplication or overlap.

Department of Labor (DOL)

Government agency that audits ERISA plans.

Dollar Cost Averaging

When you buy a fixed dollar amount of shares of mutual funds at regular intervals in all market cycles, when the market is moving down as well as when the market is moving up.

Effective Tax Rate

The percentage of tax you actually pay on your Adjusted Gross Income (AGI) after deductions are applied.

Efficient Market

The market does what it does, perfectly and randomly, without forecasting, second-guessing or intervention because all information is available to all participants and prices respond immediately to available information.

Employee Retirement Income Security Act (ERISA)

The law that underlies the basic rules for employee benefit plans. ERISA also establishes standards of conduct for fiduciaries.

Exchange Traded Funds (ETFs)

Investments similar to index funds; however, less diversified and more costly than institutional asset class mutual funds.

Financial Freedom

Not depending on anyone else or any government program for your lifestyle needs. To do as you please when you please.

Free Markets Philosophy

A fundamental core belief that prices of services and goods are arranged completely by the mutual and free consent of sellers and buyers. Markets are random and unpredictable.

Free Market Coach a.k.a. Wealth Coach, Investment Coach, Financial Coach, etc.

A type of registered investment advisory representative who advises you on achieving your dreams, throughout all the stages of your life, earns a tax-deductible advisory fee, and uses the Free Market philosophy.

Money Manager

Manages and diversifies your funds and correlates the institutional asset class mutual funds with your risk tolerances and investment objectives, the results of the goals and virtues you have established with your Free Market Coach.

Front Load

Mutual funds that charge a commission or a sales charge each time you purchase shares, sometimes called "units."

Gap

Income needed but not covered by other retirement income.

General Partner (GP)

Manages the Limited Partnership program and must send out a k-1 each year to the Limited Partners.

Giving

Sharing something with others without any requirement or expectation of reciprocity. We believe that giving is mandatory for absolute happiness and fulfillment and it can be addictive.

Grandfathered

When the government changes laws, they typically allow the previous laws and commitments made during the previous laws to hold, calling them "Grandfathered." However, when the laws change and they backdate the changes to a certain date before the commitments, the previous commitments are *not* Grandfathered.

Growth Stock Funds

Mutual funds that hold stocks of various companies with fast growing earnings, for capital appreciation.

Hedge Funds

Higher risk and mostly unregulated funds that are somewhat illiquid and difficult to keep track of. If this type of fund changes its investment objective, and it can, it is hard to react quickly enough to get out.

Hidden Costs

Expenses and detrimental activities you cannot see within the investment's financial transaction process, administration and workings.

House Funds

Mutual funds created by large broker dealers, also called proprietary funds. These investments typically pay larger commissions to the Advisor and generally have poorer returns.

Illiquid

Money you cannot use because it is invested in something you cannot easily sell or has a penalty, a surrender charge, or a maturity date. Illiquidity creates lost opportunities.

Information Overload

Stress induced by the false feeling that you need to know everything before making a decision. The result is that you become paralyzed in your actions to avoid making a mistake. Therefore you do nothing.

Institutional Asset Class Mutual Funds

A fee-only mutual fund that holds only one level of stock or bond asset class. This type of fund could have larger investment minimums.

Investment Company

A public company organized to invest in securities and hires a money manager to select and manage the securities in the portfolio.

Investment Philosophy (IP)

How you believe the market works. There are two philosophies: Active Money Management (Markets Fail) or Passive Money Management (Markets Work). Once your IP belief is determined and written down, you will know what investment strategy is appropriate for you to use to accomplish your goals.

Investment Premium

An extra investment return for taking appropriate additional risk.

Investment Strategy

The method used to implement your investment philosophy, in order to accomplish your goals.

Limited Partnership (LP)

An illiquid investment where a group of investors purchase real estate or equipment to be run by a General Partner. Investors are called Limited Partners, as they have no say in the management of the program. This is a 15 to 25-year program. Some limited partnerships turn out to be lifetime investments.

Management Charges

Charges made by the managers of, for example, a mutual fund or unit trust which cover investment management and administration costs. Charges usually take the form of a percentage fee based on the value of the fund.

Market Impact

Pressure on a stock price while broker executes the trade. This can be positive or negative.

Market Maker

A company or an individual, that quotes both a buy and a sell price in a financial instrument or commodity held in inventory, hoping to make a profit on the bid-offer spread.

Market Timing

An abusive strategy that active money managers use. Choosing to get in and out of the market or allowing someone else to decide when to move your money between the different asset classes or sectors based on various factors such as economic forecasts, interest rates, and other market conditions.

Missed Trades

When the broker fails to execute your trade during an upward price cycle.

Modern Portfolio Theory (MPT)

The only investment strategy that won the Nobel Prize in economics in 1990. The theory attempts to maximize portfolio expected return for a given amount of portfolio risk, or equivalently minimize risk for a given level of expected return, by carefully choosing the proportions of various assets.

Parable of the Talents

Jesus' story about the Master who gave out talents, a form of money. Those who squandered their talents had them taken away from them, and those who used their talents and made more talents were rewarded with additional talents.

Peace of Mind

Pure contentment and happiness with what you have, and have not done.

Policy

A contract, typically with an insurance company.

Proprietary

Investments created for the broker dealer's advisors to sell, typically mutual funds and insurance. Also called "house" products. These products typically pay a larger commission to the Advisor and have poorer results for the Investor.

Random Market

Good things happen (Berlin Wall torn down) and bad things happen (9/11) worldwide, and they all affect the market, which adjusts quickly to new information. No human knows or can predict the future—it is unpredictable, or random.

Real Estate Investment Trusts (REITS)

Illiquid real estate programs that have a limited lifespan. Many typically plan to go "public" in approximately five years but many times last much longer.

Rebalancing

Assets that outperform beyond their set targets need their gains sold off and reinvested into the under-performing target asset classes. This process maintains appropriate portfolio weightings and offsets losses. Rebalancing follows the #1 rule of investing, buy low and sell high.

Retail Mutual Funds

Mutual funds you purchase on a load or no-load basis typically using an 800 number or from other Advisors, such as commission-based representatives or stockbrokers. Some retail funds have surrender charges.

Retirement Plan Fiduciary

An entity held responsible for implementing the ERISA rules and is also held accountable when the Department of Labor does their audit. The fiduciary is typically the employer, management, and the employee investment committee.

Risk

Probability that the return on an investment will be lower than expected a/k/a the standard deviation or volatility of an investment. A good risk is one that can be managed and that will reasonably compensate the Investor over time, according to the level of volatility the Investor feels comfortable with.

Sectors

Divisions of various areas of focus within an asset class, such as industrial, financial, manufacturing, etc.

U.S. Securities and Exchange Commission (SEC)

The governmental regulator over the investment industry and all public companies.

Standard Deviation

A measure of the dispersion of a set of data from its mean. The more spread apart the data, the higher the deviation. Standard deviation is applied to the annual rate of return of an investment to measure the investment's volatility or risk.

Stress

Emotional and physical reactions to situations which sometime results in activity that creates worry and frustration. Stress can make you physically ill.

Steward

A manager or trustee of 100% of the assets God has blessed you with.

Stock Picking

An abusive active money management strategy that picks and invests in individual stocks, resulting in limited diversification and higher risk, due to gambling and speculating with your money.

Stock Picking Game

A game used in middle schools and high schools to teach students about the market. It focuses on buying and selling stocks, which is active trading.

Surrender Fee

A penalty for exiting an insurance policy or investment early, before its maturity date.

Target percentages

What the money manager sets for each of your Free Market portfolio's risk levels, or asset classes. Rebalancing uses the target percentages.

Third-Party Administrator (TPA)

An administrator of an ERISA retirement plan outside your financial Advisors' company, completely independent from your money manager, investment company, fee Advisor and employer. It is responsible for the day-to-day administration of your retirement plan.

Track Record Investing

An abusive strategy that active money managers use. It is the process of looking at how an investment has done historically over time, and then deciding to invest in it because of its previous track record. Past performance is no guarantee of future results.

Trades

Buying or selling of investments such as stocks, bonds or mutual funds.

Turnover

The frequency of the buying and selling of bonds or stocks within a mutual fund. Every time there is a buy or sell, whether you approve it or not, expenses are charged to your account. You pay for those trading costs, whether you have or have not approved the sales and purchases. The lower the turnover, the lower your investment costs.

Value Stock Funds

A mutual fund made up of distressed growth stock that a money manager believes are undervalued in the market.

WIN-LOSE

The investment company, possibly a day trading company, wins and the day trading Investor loses, as there is a charge every time his money is moved, whether he makes money or not.

WIN-WIN-LOSE

The Advisor and investment or insurance company win by making money and the Investor loses money.

WIN-WIN-WIN

No one is abused or taken advantage of. All expectations are met, so everyone wins, typically the Investor, Coach and ministry!

Worry

A waste of your precious time.

Learn More About Stress-Free Investing!

Free Market Videos
Wealth Coaching Videos
Stewardship Coaching Videos
Talk to a Free Market Coach

616-460-6518

www.Stress-FreeInvesting.com
www.WordhouseWealthCoaching.com
info@WordhouseWealthCoaching.com

*What good is it for a man to gain the whole world,
and yet lose or forfeit his very self?*

– Luke 9:25

CPSIA information can be obtained at www.ICGtesting.com
Printed in the USA
BVOW011213170313

315676BV00009B/198/P